Preface

These lectures, given at the Collège International de Philosophie in Paris in 2004–2005, were intended to unravel the shift from modernity to postmodernity as analyzed in political science and philosophy. Their point of departure was the attempt to work out the political language that corresponded to such a transition. At the time, I had considered the following title: *For a New Grammar of Politics*. Was I successful in tracing a few leads, defining concepts and new categories that could express the change affecting us today? I leave it to the reader to decide.

The lecture program was conceived as follows:

The Modern and the Postmodern. Whenever we speak of something that is "between the modern and the postmodern," we imply a mutation in the discourse on politics. We will first research and define the concept of democracy in the postmodern period, by which we mean the collection of cultural forms, ideological labels and institutional mechanisms that have arisen subsequently to the crisis of the nation-state, and that partake in the process of forming imperial sovereignty.

Biopowers and Biopolitics. Second, we will chart the differences between the political concepts of the modern state and those of postmodern Empire. These differences are essentially articulated around the dimension of *Bios* and its grounding at the heart of the definition of politics. We shall confront the different conceptions of biopolitics, by taking into consideration both their genesis and their effects, and finally insist on the fundamental difference between biopowers and biopolitics.

New Political Lexicon. Third, we will attempt to open a theoretical discussion on the possibility of a new political lexicon. The aim will be to redefine, within the postmodern horizon and in relation to the political contradictions that have emerged there, key concepts such as sovereignty, citizenship, rights, the common, the individual, the collective, private/public, peace, war, the multitude, constituent power, etc.

I had embarked on a similar endeavor in recent years, through a series of lectures given at La Sapienza University in Rome, as well as conferences given in Catalonia and at the Mellon Foundation in Pittsburg. The project had come about as an attempt to show that a new definition of politics was possible, even if it was not easy. The publication of two of my books in Italy, now translated here and there, *Guide* and *Movimenti nell'Impero* (Raffaello Cortina Editore, 2002 and 2006), had inaugurated the debate.

Undoubtedly, this research came up against certain obstacles less due to the logic and deployment of the project itself than to rather strong exterior political opposition. In my work environment—that is to say, in the cultural and political Left to which I belong, despite the vagaries of my personal path—changing political perspectives and new conceptual definitions of the parameters of such modifications have often been very ill received. In Italy and Spain, Germany and Great Britain, such difficulties were somewhat relative: the debate occurred, and was often fruitful, even if polemical.

SEMIOTEXT(E) FOREIGN AGENTS SERIES

© 2008 Semiotext(e)
© Éditions Stock, 2006

Published by Semiotext(e)
2007 Wilshire Blvd., Suite 427, Los Angeles, CA 90057
www.semiotexte.com

Special thanks to Jessica Eckert, and Robert Dewhurst.

Cover art by Jason Rhoades
Installation view at CAC Malaga, Malaga, Spain of *Tijuanatanjierchandelier*, 2006. Courtesy Estate of Jason Rhoades; Galerie Hauser & Wirth, London and Zurich; David Zwirner, New York.
Photography by José Luis Gutiérrez.

Backcover photography by Marco Dotti
Design by Hedi El Kholti

ISBN: 978-1-58435-056-9
Distributed by The MIT Press, Cambridge, Mass. and London, England
Printed in the United States of America

THE PORCELAIN WORKSHOP

FOR A NEW GRAMMAR OF POLITICS

Antonio Negri

Translated by Noura Wedell

\<e\>

Contents

In Germany and in Great Britain in particular, the interest, participation, and commitment to the discussions were remarkable.

In France, things went quite differently. I was meant to start these lectures in early October 2004, thanks to the interest and the warm welcome that the project received from the Collège International de Philosophie. I had to reschedule the first session because of a bad flu. The following week, the conference room was full, but I was compelled to suspend the seminar almost immediately: loud shouts were coming from a group of people who had mingled with the public with the sole intent of preventing the meeting. I dislike not understanding something—and I tried, as usual, to understand the reasons for such violence. I was accused of being an imperialist lackey because I questioned socialist categories. I was denounced as a cheat because I was trying to reinvent a communist perspective for the years to come. They called me all sorts of names and accused me of treason. It was quite incomprehensible, quite vulgar as well—and gauging the irony of the situation required a considerable amount of humor: I had spent a good number of years in prison only to be told I was a traitor and had to fall back on Spinoza in order to laugh at these *ultimi barbarorum*.

The protests continued for a few sessions, then abated. They reappeared when I announced my support for the campaign for a "yes" vote during the referendum on the European Constitutional Treaty. It seemed to me at the time—and does so today even more—that only in Europe can we build a political field that corresponds to the most recent transformations of social conflictuality, rendering the latter strategically essential for a genuine politics of multitudes on a globalized scale.

What name should I have given this book? *Ten lessons for an angry public—with the desire to convince?* I must admit I seriously considered it. The situation also reminded me of similar events in the mid 1980s that arose when I first opened the vocabulary of the Left to discussion. At the time, just as I was beginning my exile in Paris, a short book of mine had come out in a limited edition in Italy. It was entitled *Fabbriche del soggetto*—which we could translate in French as *Subject Factories*, or, even worse, but perhaps more precisely, *Subject Manufactures*. Why not call the new book, twenty years later, *Subject Manufactures no 2*? Wasn't it the second part of a project, initiated at the time, to formulate the necessity of reestablishing political language according to the transformations of the political field?

Unfortunately, the title did not sound good—and the esthetically unsound is never scientifically useful! In addition, the problem was not to provide "manufactured" concepts, as manufacture seemed to imply, but to sense the becoming of a conceptual transformation that would have a much greater impact.

In reality, I had two things in mind. The first was a joint invitation to all scholars of good will to work on a new postmodern vocabulary of the political field. What a wonderful experience that could be! The invitation still stands and is more important than ever. Secondly, it was necessary to accept the kind of "double truth" we must inevitably face when we attempt to modify the axes and terms of left-wing politics. This "double truth" is what brings us to say things differently according to our interlocutor. Today, it does not come out of hatred for our enemy—as was the case in medieval history—but out of love for friendship. I am convinced that our discourse must be open to socialists and communists who have lived honestly, and who have conceived of their own experience according to the old dialectical terms of Marxism-Leninism. They are the ones, above all, who must be accompanied in *this discovery of a new field of inquiry and struggles*, just as in our youth they accompanied us to the factories, in the workers' struggle, and offered us the wealth of communist knowledge.

Ethics is more important here than logic. It makes no difference if logic functions according to the regime of "double truth." Of course, this does not hold universally. Yet it is sufficient that it hold for us today, in the transition that is ours. At a time when the choice to become multitude, and construct a political horizon of radical change, comes from the need to invent a new language on par with our expectations, and able to follow the movements of our desire: a language that can trace with renewed vigor the fluid line of the Marxian curve.

It might be objected that this could provide the powerful with better tools of domination. I am not afraid. Capitalists and the reactionary Right, as experience shows, are less intelligent than they ought to be.

We thus advanced in the project. These lectures gradually became small conceptual "work-groups" of shared reflection and common knowledge. We might have preferred the climate to be sometimes more serene, less violently conflictual, less brutal. Very often, however, it was extremely gratifying: even the fiercest discussions were conducted as a debate without prejudice.

It was a passionate debate, full of expectations, yet fragile still. At the beginning of this preface, I was speaking of the different titles I had thought of for the book. Putting aside my scruples and doubts, I chose *The Porcelain Workshop*, and those who know of my clumsiness will laugh at the image. However, we are not speaking simply of the grace of the elephant in the china shop. In these lessons, we can feel a shared breath but also a great wind, rattling those who exist in this strange world of ours, weakening hopes, attempts, expectations, and movements. It is a great wind: it is up to us to make it like those spring breezes that whip our faces but leave the sky clear and nature vivified so that the powers of new life and victorious struggles can be affirmed.

— *Paris, April 2006.*

Modern and Postmodern: the Caesura

The political categories of modernity, that is, theories of government, are open to a strong and decided critique. Accordingly, in the following sessions, we will devote ourselves to the elaboration of a new vocabulary and a new grammar of contemporary politics.

We must first remark, in the modern period, the striking homogeneity between a number of very different positions. Indeed, in Max Weber, Carl Schmitt, and Lenin, power is interpreted as *univocal*. It is always transcendent, always sovereign; power is a sovereign machine. For Max Weber, a proponent of liberal-functionalism, for Carl Schmitt, who interprets a conservative and totalitarian tradition, and finally, for Lenin, who represents an exceptional revolutionary moment whose goal is the extinction of the bourgeois state, power is given, in an acutely homologous definition, as transcendent, an arcanum.

We must insist on this point: even when confronted with a quasi-anarchic conception of politics, and when the liberation of the proletariat coincides with the disappearance of the state—as it does for Lenin—the whole of political reasoning is in fact closely taken up in a dialectical relation with existing power and its sovereign definition. This entails a single alternative that we can formulate as follows: either one takes power, taking on the characteristics of power, or one renounces power absolutely and the possibility of political space is immediately defined as the absolute negation of power. There is no intermediary solution, and both cases lead to a dead end. Stretching from the end of the nineteenth century to the beginning of the twentieth, state theoreticians (from Rudolf Stammler in Germany to Emile Durkheim in France) could not escape this alternative—the Reich or the Republic on one side, anarchy on the other—and remained its prisoners.

Let us examine with greater precision *the vast homology of the conceptions of power in modern thought*. We shall start with Max Weber's *Politik als Beruf* (*Politics as a Vocation*), and try to follow its line of reasoning. The transcendence of power is represented by Weber's use of quasi-religious language to analyze the actions of political subjects. Politics is not a condition but a vocation. In this perspective, the relativism and polytheism of political values that Weber defends become figures of the passage from political experience to the transcendence of power. They are figures of the neutralization of the ontological dimension of politics. Power becomes a reality to adhere to, something that gives itself beyond reality, a calling, or eventually, martyrdom...

Weber's epistemological neo-Kantianism (the idea that political determinations are categorical) must then be reinvested within a thought of transcendence—a kind of lay faith—that ends up betraying both the *Critique of Pure Reason* and the *Critique of Practical Reason*. It comes as no surprise that Weber is now read essentially as a Nietzschean author: both for his realist pessimist position on political experience, and for his "negative thought" concerning the idea of salvation as exclusively linked to autonomy or to the untimeliness of political decision. The great epoch of the functionalist readings of Weber *à la* Talcott Parsons is over (some, like Raymond Aron, had been arguing the weakness of such projects for a long time). These theoretical episodes clearly show how the Platonic tradition is maintained in the modern expression of power and of the political field.

From this point of view, Nietzsche offers an impure and ambiguous reading, that both opens and closes the relation between the reality and ideality of power while always maintaining the latter's transcendence. If Nietzsche's interpretation of the world is pessimistic, if nature must acknowledge the waste of its possibilities and history the destruction of its powers, it is because reality must henceforth—and precisely in a "realistic" manner—bend to the logical necessities of the management and reproduction of power. Inside the Platonic cave, the world appears a relativised shadow that can only be understood by domination.

In Weber's liberal and functional perspective on power, the concept of the political is constructed from above, through closure and through necessity: from above because power is transcendent; through closure because power, inasmuch as it is One, by definition excludes all differences; through necessity, for it cannot be otherwise. As we shall show, this perspective anticipates the idea of biopower Foucault starts developing in the 1970s. The three modalities of the construction of political power listed above could very well apply to the political permeation of life by the state, and more generally, to the micropower network crisscrossing the totality of what determines our existence. In both cases, in Weber and in the Foucauldian analysis of biopower, we are confronted with power as a homologized and homologizing figure. But, contrary to Weber, Foucault does not rest there.

If we analyze Carl Schmitt, we are faced, paradoxically enough, with a concept quite analogous to Max Weber's. From this point of view, it is very difficult to identify the first as a democratic thinker and the second as a totalitarian one. Both confuse the theoretical definition of power with the subjective dimension that should define it. Schmitt and Weber differ on the terrain of constitutional theory, but are quite close in terms of political theory. Schmitt also conceives of politics as mystical and theological. Without Weber's Kantian transcendental cover, his power is simply a drastic reduction of ethics to politics. He makes no distinction between an ethics of conviction and one of responsibility; rather, there is a totalitarian flow linking one to the other.

As many contemporary writers from Foucault to Agamben have demonstrated, *biopower* (power's pervasion of the totality of life) and *totalitarianism* (pervasion of the totality of life by the state) operate on a shared terrain, at least partially. German law created a monster within the European constitutional theories of what Foucault would much later qualify as biopolitical. Biopower as totalitarianism: the result of nineteenth and twentieth century struggles, the construction of *welfare*, the social dimension of consensus have all been absorbed by the totality of the state.

National Socialism is the dramatic fulfillment of this figure, and politics is, for Carl Schmitt, the space of its reality. For Schmitt, power is in fact a sort of totalitarian panopticon: each citizen lives inside the living God, the panopticon becomes pantheism. Unlike a panoptic system, however, this living God must also define out-casts: these are precisely outcasts from life, those whose life will soon be declared worthless. *Aufhebung*, the dialectical resolution of this process—leaving behind those whose life is worthless—translates as the expansion of living space and corresponds to what we would call *Nation Building* today. Once again, an alleged universal construction, in reality subjects its citizens... Such is the good work of the reactionary mole.

The problem of decision—that seems, at first glance, to concern individuals, as only individuals decide—*takes the place of transcendent asceticism in the Weberian calling.* In both cases, what is constructed is a place where the individual can distribute gifts to friends and inflict death on enemies... It is not surprising that war (as a decision of the sovereign *and* as the unveiling of the nature of the political) reveals the intimate workings of biopower and its absolute untimeliness. War deprives citizens of the possibility of political decision, while maintaining an absolute grasp on their existence. Clausewitz's famous dictum that war is the continuation of politics by other means was not taken up by the neoconservatives in the 1990s but by the Fascists and Schmittians of the 1930s—and as Foucault would say, even before that, by nineteenth century liberals.

For Lenin, in *The State of the Revolution*, the conception of politics is just as anchored in transcendence, as the identification that some theorists have argued of the Leninist decision with the Schmittian one goes to show... Not that carrying out revolutionary politics automatically instates the reign of transcendence. On the contrary, the revolutionary action of the proletariat dissolves transcendence at the same time as politics. For Lenin, the disappearance of the state is an anarchic ideal exactly symmetrical to, and inverting, state transcendence as understood by bourgeois theorists. The idea of the liberation of the proletariat is completely engaged in a dialectical relation to power.

To repeat, in both the cases we have just seen, we are faced with a double impasse that seems to impose a necessary choice between two possibilities. The first consists in taking power and becoming *another* power, that is to say, inescapably remaining *a power*. The second attempts to totally deny the power exerted over life, and therefore emerges as a negation of life itself. From this point of view, the concept of proletarian power that we find in Lenin is completely symmetrical to that of bourgeois power. The concept of liberation is caught in the vise of power. *Might we not imagine, on the contrary, that freedom, singularity and potency* (puissance) *come about as radical differences from power?*

Let us clarify this point so as not to attribute errors to Lenin that were not his own. Lenin is perfectly conscious of the impasse in which he finds himself. In fact, after posing the problem of insurrection and of the destruction of power, he insists on its dualism, on transition and the dictatorship of the proletariat as a form of commanding the transition itself. Lenin is not responsible for the liberticidal practices committed in his name. (And who can clearly ascertain that other avenues were available at the time? What is certain is that there are alternatives today and that it is our duty to embark upon them.)

If we want to shatter the bourgeois capitalist conception of power, we must go beyond the modern conception of power itself.

It is useful, however, to stress that the modern cannot be reduced to merely these political categories. An alternative exists in modern thought (Machiavelli versus theories of *"raison d'Etat,"* Spinoza versus Hobbes) that stands in opposition to what we have just seen, and gives reasons for political association and for the democratic dynamic against transcendental conceptions of power. It affirms the immanence of politics and the constitutive and constituent dimension of democracy. The concepts of multitude and democracy in use in the debate at hand were born of this perspective.

This is what I attempted to show about Spinoza in my book, *The Savage Anomaly*.[1]

We will therefore try to demonstrate that the political situation we are faced with today can only be defined *within a paradigm shift in relation to the modern tradition*. We intend to show in particular that it is easier to define the contemporary as postmodern than as hypermodern, in spite of the changes the term has undergone particularly in France and in the United States.

Many theoreticians, sociologists, and politicians—I am mainly thinking here of certain German intellectuals such as Ulrich Beck—have labeled the contemporary period *hypermodern* all the while paradoxically thinking it in continuous relation to the modern tradition. We will try to prove that only a paradigm shift can allow us to interpret the contemporary period, particularly in regards to themes of power, work, and globalization. We insist on this paradigm shift for it affirms a discontinuity that is a starting point, and must be acknowledged. This radical caesura is an essential component of the discussion we wish to engage.

In fact, one cannot address the issue of the caesura without mentioning the crisis of modernity (that is to say, of its political categories), derived from a long series of phenomena.

Let us, for example, ask what it means to "work" today. For a long time, work was reduced to the production of material goods. Today, "work" refers to the entirety of social activity. In order to understand this mutation, we must keep in mind the struggles and transformations of the organization of labor since 1917, an

---

1. Negri, Antonio. *The Savage Anomaly: The Power of Spinoza's Metaphysics and Politics.* Translation Michael Hardt. Minneapolis: University of Minnesota Press, 1991.

insurrectional challenge on the part of the workers that, for the long term (what some, precisely, have labeled the "short century"), plunged the whole of organized labor into crisis. The first response to the aggression of living work towards the capitalist system took the form of the *New Deal*, and then developed as the general spread of the *welfare state* in the central regions of the planet, through the imposition of biopolitical forms of organization and exploitation of both society and the state.

It has since become impossible to define social and productive activity in terms of the modern socialist tradition. Today, we face a tendency towards the hegemony of immaterial work (intellectual, scientific, cognitive, relational, communicative, affective, etc.) increasingly characterizing both the mode of production and processes of valorization. It goes without saying that this form of work is entirely subordinate to new modes of accumulation and exploitation. We can no longer interpret these according to the classic labor theory of value that measures work according to the time employed in production. Cognitive work is not measurable in those terms; it is even characterized by its immensurability, its *excess* (*excédence*). A productive relation links cognitive work to the time of life. It is nourished by life as much as it modifies it in return, and its products are those of freedom and imagination. This creativity is precisely the excess that characterizes it. Of course, work still remains at the center of the entire process of production (and this is where we affirm our *fidelity to Marxism*), but its definition cannot be reduced to a purely material or labor dimension. This constitutes the *first element of the caesura* between the modern and the postmodern.

A second caesura occurs in regards to the redefinition of the very notion of sovereignty. Under the management of the *welfare state*, the processes that organize social work have invested society as a whole. Sovereign action has become progressively defined as a growing biopower spreading to cover the entire social field. We have moved from the discipline of the individual organization of labor to the control of populations. The process of *real subsumption of society under capital* here expresses itself in all its glory. The distinction between formal subsumption and real subsumption of society under capital goes back to Marx. At the stage of formal subsumption, capital marshals different forms of production under its command: handicraft, peasant, industrial, etc. The capitalist commandment thus presents itself from the outside as the unifying force of all these differences. In real subsumption, however, all forms of production are defined from the outset as homogenous in order to allow for profit. Capital, in this case, is limited to harnessing and accumulating social work. In Foucaldian terms, we have moved from a disciplinarian regime to a regime of control. To clarify this point, please allow me to refer to Marx's pages in the sixth unpublished chapter of Book I of the *Capital,* and in *Grundisse,* as well as to André Gorz's recent works.

The biopolitical government of society thus consequently tends towards totalitarianism. Biopolitics can even go so far as verging on thanatopolitics: biopolitics and thanatopolitics tend to identify occasionally, as war becomes the essence of politics, and thanatopolitics the matrix of biopolitics.

What interests us here above all is *the reversal, as paradoxical as it is dramatic, that is playing itself out.* For we rapidly discover that *the global extension of capitalist power over society corresponds to the global spread of insubordination.* How are we justified in affirming this? When the law of value—that commands capitalist development—comes to fail, then the capacity of capital to contain the productive force of labor (immaterial, cognitive, affective, linguistic, etc.) in itself also wears out. Ignorance in regards to the new quality of work and the preoccupation of capitalist command must now face new insubordination and social resistance. The general situation is therefore predisposed to antagonism. This is the second ground on which we can define the radical difference between modernity and the contemporary period.

The third series of phenomena concerns the globalization of economic processes and the crisis of the concepts of nation-state, people, sovereignty, etc., following from it. Capitalist development had found its fundamental structure in the nation-state. Today, on the contrary, it is in the crisis of the nation-state as induced by globalization that the general crisis of the political categories of modernity manifests, opening thought to the relation between Empire and the multitudes.

We will return to these elements, to the philosophical crisis of the categories of modernity and to the emergence of new concepts, in greater depth. For now, we would like to insist on the fact that the postmodern political horizon appears foremost as the dissolution of the political ontology built around the concept of sovereignty. Not only are the categories of sovereignty affected, reality itself emerges transformed. It is therefore on this point that the political theories of the modern encounter their definitive limit. We discover that sovereignty can no longer be a reduction to the One. Such a reduction being no longer possible, the exercise of sovereignty must affront irreducible differences and submit itself to a ceaselessly growing antagonism. From this line of tension and of explicit antagonism, by recuperating the Machiavellian theory of "tumult," by making ours the Spinozan theory of democratic "multitude" and the Marxist theory of the "class struggle," we can start to define the specific, singular characteristics of our times.

During the course of these lectures, we will also attempt to confront other philosophical theories that have reflected on this mutation of the paradigm of modernity. We have seen how important it is to insist on the depth of the caesura at hand, the rupture induced by the biopolitical order in relation to modern reflections on power. We have just lived through a long crisis warning us against the *great narratives* of historical development. Those attempting them, beware! It was a difficult condition to overcome. It has become increasingly evident that biopower, between the end of the nineteenth and the beginning of the twentieth century, developed as subjugation of all conditions of life, and that life was at the heart of the productive process, representing its absolute condition of possibility. Today, there are many ways to arrive at such knowledge: from the point of view of a day laborer demanding a guaranteed salary or of an IT engineer needing freeware; from the point of view of a stay at home parent or of a student requiring more time for training and education. In all of these cases, men's and women's lives constitute the base of the valorization process, and inversely, valorization permeates their existence: the objective and the subjective identify completely. Why isn't such an incredible change in the social and productive context recognized? And once it is recognized, why not remunerate life itself, taking stock of the fact that each individual is productive, simply by living in a productive society? As a matter of fact, the demand for indirect salaries and for services that are adequate to the reproduction of society as a whole has become widespread. We found it necessary, regarding this issue, to introduce the Marxist concept of *real subsumption of society under capital*. The reader may recall that the Marxian definition of real subsumption of society under capital not only implies that this society corresponds entirely to merchandise, but also that the contradiction and antagonism determined by the production of merchandise has invested *the whole of* society. Consequently, general remuneration corresponds to the general dimensions of antagonism in social production.

Now, the Frankfurt School had perfectly grasped and described this situation. It was at the root of the general (and, in a certain sense, quite spectacular) circulation of the notion of real subsumption in postmodern thought (from this point of view, Adorno and Horkheimer's *Dialectic of Enlightenment* had already anticipated a thousand texts on postmodernism). At the beginning, the postmodern seemed the limitless illustration of this subsumption. But the postmodern is not simply a new way of thinking: it is also a concrete redefinition of the real. Some thinkers, however, could only connect the real perception of what was happening to an ironic and superficial consciousness of its process. Although somewhat "pretty," this period was enormously irresponsible: it was the reign of "weak" thought, of generalized philosophical and historical revisionism, of the aestheticizing translation of weighty Heideggerian ontology. It is well known that every historical moment possesses both comic and tragic characteristics. In the case at hand, it took a while for the tragic to emerge once again from behind the fragile dancing figures of a postmodernity without consistency. This is precisely where we position ourselves: between a full yet philosophically fragile conception of real subsumption, and the tragic moment when the first insurgent critiques were produced.

In postmodernity, the critique of real subsumption underwent a difficult training period. In the following lectures, we will try to analyze these periods with care. A first phase was characterized by the perception that *there could be no alternative* to the subsumption of society under capital and to the biopower that constituted its political structure—except for marginal resistance. Jacques Derrida chose precisely to act on the margins, on marginal excess, by transforming the philosophy of the gift into a philosophy of waiting and friendship. Giorgio Agamben tried to reclaim, in a naturalist and extreme manner, the problems of innovation and of the figure of the gap. Finally, with Jean-Luc Nancy, marginal tension took the form of a nascent common... Now, in all of these readings, we find reproduced the image of a certain *dialectical and paradoxical univocity* of the resistance/power relation. Power always determines the foreign where resistance can take place... When resistance ceases to appear on the central stage of historical development (as in the Hegelian tradition, particularly in its left-wing version) and is relegated on the contrary to a marginal, synchronic, and transversal dimension, we can no longer perceive an *idea of potency* (puissance), a position of antagonism or an instance of liberation. Apparently, the only solution remains the star of redemption or that of messianic time. As for us, we refuse to return to the fleeting shadows of that desperate generation.

One last remark on that matter. There is no *outside* to our world of real subsumption of society under capital. We live within it, but it has no exterior; we are engulfed in commodity fetishism—without recourse to something that might represent its transcendence. Nature and humanity have been transformed by capital. From now on, all aspirations to alterity (as in the important tradition stretching from Rosa Luxemburg to Walter Benjamin) are not only outdated but also vain. And yet: from inside this fetishistic world, the antagonism of living work is affirming itself and resistance is building.

The problem of reclaiming freedom within the very circle of power must be addressed—and this, just as power has become a biopower that nothing seems to be able to stop.

There is no doubt that the world defined by the real subsumption of society under capital coagulates and neutralizes possibilities of relations, but it does not do this to resistance, to freedom as potency (puissance) or to the constitution of new being. In the same was as factory workers struggled against the direct exploitation of the assembly line, today, in a society put to work as a whole, the multitudes are rising. It is precisely between Foucault and Deleuze that *the passage from the margin to the center of the block of biopower* occurred, and that resistance became an ontological force. Foucault gives us a definition of biopower, reformulating and historicizing the analyses of the Frankfurt School, along with a definition of an active biopolitics. He also pinpoints the progressive emergence of a process of production of subjectivities capable of transforming subjects both in themselves, and in their relation to power. In Deleuze, the examination and periodization of the different phases of the relation between biopower and biopolitical reality—from discipline to control—reestablishes the ontological determination of resistance within the historical grid of real subsumption. Thus, the postmodern is given not only through the caesura it creates with modernity but also through the new conditions of an antagonistic process. The latter invests the world of real subsumption and presents it as a world where the antagonistic forces of power and resistance, capital and freedom are at play. If we consider resistance and freedom as material bases, they must of course be defined as activities, as living work, as the production of subjectivity—that is to say, as *the invention of a new "use value"* inside power, and as the objective saturation of exchange value. But we shall return to this soon.

In short, we could say that *postmodern thought* appears under three essential philosophical forms:

a. As a philosophical reaction to the ontology of modernity and *an acknowledgment of the real subsumption of society under capital* that finds no other outlet than a "slack" thought and weak contractualism. We refer, for example, to the works of Jean-François Lyotard, Jean Baudrillard, Gianni Vattimo, or Richard Rorty... We are here in a kind of Marxist heresy that reduces subjectivity to mercantile circulation, that erases all references to use value and fixes the equivalence of production and circulation.

b. As *marginal resistance*, as the oscillation between a kind of "commodity fetishism" and the pull of mystical eschatology. Here we find Jacques Derrida, Jean-Luc Nancy, and Giorgio Agamben. The last two seem to reintroduce Benjamin's communist utopia on the margins of real subsumption.

c. As critical postmodernism, in other words, as *the acknowledgment* not only of our historical phase but also of *the antagonism that corresponds to it*. And consequently: as the reconstruction of a *space of subjectivation*. We are speaking here essentially of Michel Foucault and Gilles Deleuze.

We have just provided the preliminary elements of what will constitute our object of study and analysis in the following workshops. There will be ten such workshops: the second will address the definition of the biopolitical; the third will analyze the dissolution of national sovereignty and themes of war and peace; the fourth will attempt to define the notion of the common beyond issues of public and private; the fifth will address the critique of postmodernism; the sixth shall concentrate on resistance and differences; in the seventh, eighth, and ninth, we shall pause to consider those themes that characterize the critique of modern theories of government; finally, in the last lecture, we shall confront the most essential philosophical knot of this passage from the modern to the postmodern, in other words, the alternatives of temporality, measure, and common freedom.

The Work of the Multitude

and the Biopolitical Fabric

I would like this session to address the manner in which the organization of labor—and of the new postmodern political field that follows from it—is grounded in the *Bios*. In a moment, we shall see *how and when life enters into the field of power and becomes a major stake therein.*

In the first lecture, we insisted on the homology of the political categories of modern thought in the work of thinkers as diverse as Max Weber, Carl Schmitt, and Lenin. We also emphasized how strongly an opposition inherent to the history of political philosophy affected the political categories of modernity: Machiavelli versus Machiavellianism and theories of "*raison d'Etat*," Spinoza versus Hobbes. Finally, we showed how the crisis of modern thought was linked to three larger series of causes: the metamorphosis of the organization of labor; the biopolitical anchoring of sovereignty, that is, the way techniques of sovereignty have passed from the exercise of discipline to that of control; the general crisis of categories following the globalization process.

We started with a discussion of the philosophical forms through which the crisis of modernity and the apparition of the new postmodern paradigm came to be expressed. We critiqued those positions insisting on commodity fetishism and on the equivalence of production and circulation in the new circuit of capital (often called the "weak theories" of postmodernity) as well as the diverse schools of thought that sought to oppose marginal resistance to the emergence of the postmodern (the "ontologies of the margin" and the various "neo-Benjaminian" readings). We recognized, on the contrary, in theories concerning the production of subjectivity (Foucault and Deleuze) *a decisive moment* for the reconstruction of a critical project.

Let us take *the Foucaldian definition of biopolitics* as a starting point. The term "biopolitics" indicates the way power, at a certain point, transforms itself to govern not only individuals, through a certain number of disciplinary processes, but also humanity constituted in "populations." Biopolitics (through local biopowers) is thus concerned with the management of health, hygiene, food, birth rate, sexuality, etc., as these various fields of intervention become political stakes. In this way, biopolitics starts to engage with all the aspects of life that will become the arena for *welfare state* policies: its development is in fact wholly taken up in the attempt to better manage the labor force. Let us listen to Foucault on this point: "The discovery of population is, simultaneous to the discovery of the individual and the trainable (*dressable*) body, the other great technological node around which the political processes of the West have evolved." Biopolitics is based, therefore, on principles that develop the technologies of capitalism and sovereignty: these principles are greatly modified, in time, through their evolution from a disciplinarian form to one that adjoins to discipline the mechanisms of control. Whereas discipline was an "anatomo-politics" of bodies and essentially applied to individuals, biopolitics on the contrary represents a kind of great "social medicine" attempting the control of populations in order to govern their life: *life now belongs to the field of power.*

The notion of biopower raises two problems. The first is linked to a contradiction that we find in Foucault himself. When he first uses the term, it seems linked to what the Germans, in the eighteenth century, called *Polizeiwissenschaft*, namely, the maintenance of order and discipline through state growth and administrative organization. In later texts, however, biopolitics seems to signal the moment when the traditional state/society dichotomy is resolved in favor of a *political economy of life in general.* The other problem arises from this second formulation. Must we think of biopolitics as a collection of biopowers? Or, inasmuch as the investment of life by power means that life itself is a power, can we localize the emergence of a counter-power, the production of subjectivity as a moment of liberation (*désassujettissement*), in life itself—in work and in language, but also in bodies, affects, desires, and sexuality? Clearly, the concept of biopolitics can only be understood according to the conception that Foucault had of power itself: never a stable, coherent and unitary entity, but rather a collection of "power relations" that imply complex historical conditions and multiple effects. *Power is a field of powers.* Consequently, whenever Foucault speaks of power he is never describing a primary or fundamental principle, but rather a collection of correlations wherein practices, knowledge and institutions intersect. The concept of power is thus totally different—almost totally postmodern—in regards to the Platonic tradition whose lasting power and hegemony over a large part of modern thought we have ascertained. *Juridical models of sovereignty are subject to a political critique of the state that clearly show the circulation of power in the social body and, consequently, the variability of subjections that it gives rise to.* Paradoxically, it is precisely in the complexity of this circulation that processes of subjectivation, resistance and insubordination can occur.

Taking these different elements into account, the genesis of the concept of biopower will have to be modified according to the conditions of its appearance. For now, we shall try to emphasize the transformation at work in the organization of labor. *The periodization of labor in the industrial era* allows us to grasp the particular importance of the passage from discipline to control. We can see this passage accomplished in the *crisis of Fordism*, during which the Taylorist organization of labor could no longer discipline social movements and Keynesian macroeconomic techniques were incapable of evaluating the measure of labor. From the 1970s on, this transformation (that will in turn give rise to a redefinition of biopowers) massively takes hold in the "central" countries of capitalist development. Following the rhythm of this modification will enable us to grasp the slow problematization of the theme of the production of subjectivity in Foucault and Deleuze, emphasizing what they have in common on that issue. In Deleuze, for example, the shift in what he considers the true matrix of subjective production—no longer a network of power relations spreading throughout society but a dynamic center predisposed to subjectivation—is essential. From this point of view, on the question of discipline and control, and the definition of power it entails, Deleuze does not limit himself to interpreting Foucault but rather integrates the latter's work and develops its fundamental intuitions.

Now that we have defined biopower, without fixing and hypostasizing it, but rather in relation to a mobile history combined with the long trajectory bringing the demands of productivity to the center of the apparatuses of power, it is that history we must understand.

The danger is to read, at the heart of biopolitics, a kind of positivist vitalism (and/or materialist: in fact, we might very well be faced with what Marx called a "sad materialism"). We see this, for example, in certain recent interpretations of the political centrality of life, which read the biopolitical as a kind of confused, dangerous, and even destructive magma. This indicates a tendency towards thanatopolitics, a politics of death, rather than towards a true political affirmation of life. The shift towards thanatopolitics is, in reality, permitted and even bolstered by the great ambiguity of the word *life* itself. Under the guise of a biopolitical reflection, what we have is rather a biological and naturalizing understanding of life that strips it of all political power. Life is reduced, at best, to a heap of flesh and bones. Up to what point does Heideggerian ontology find an essential and tragic resource in this passage from the *Zoe* to the *Bios*?

The fundamental specificity of biopolitics in Foucault—the very shape of the relation between power and life—which immediately becomes, in Deleuze as well, the space of production of free subjectivity, is filtered through an indiscriminate vitalist determination. Now, as we all know, vitalism is a tenacious thing! When it starts to emerge, after the crisis of thought that occurs in the Renaissance, and in the middle of the crisis of modern thought in the seventeenth century, it paralyzes the contradictions of the world and of society, inasmuch as it considers them impossible to resolve. More precisely, these contradictions come to define the essence of the world from the postulate of their invariability. *In the haze of vitalism, there can be no discernment. Life and death are swept up in a relation of great ambiguity*: war between individuals becomes essential, and the co-presence of an aggressive animal with a society exasperated by the market—the so-called dynamic of possessive individualism—is presented as a natural norm, namely, as *life*.

Vitalism is therefore always a reactionary philosophy. Bios on the other hand, as it appears in Foucault and Deleuze's biopolitical analyses, is something else altogether; it has chosen to break with that grid of thought. For those of us thinking in their wake, biopolitics is not a return to origins, a way to ground thinking back in nature. It is rather the attempt to construct thinking from ways of life—be they individual or collective—to make thinking (and reflection on the world) spark from artificiality—understood as the refusal of all natural foundations—and the power *(puissance)* of subjectivation. *Biopolitics is neither an enigma* nor a collection of relations knotted in such an inextricable way that the immunization of life becomes the only solution. *On the contrary, it is the rediscovered terrain of all political thought,* inasmuch as it is penetrated by the power *(puissance)* of subjectivation processes.

From this point of view, the idea of biopolitics accompanies the passage of the modern into the postmodern in an essential way—if we understand the latter as the historical moment wherein power relations are interrupted by the resistance of those subjects on which they are endlessly imposed. If life has no "outside" and must consequently be lived wholly "inside," its only dynamic can be that of *potency (puissance)*. Thanatopolitics is neither an internal alternative, nor a biopolitical ambiguity. It is its exact opposite: an authoritarian transcendence, an apparatus of corruption.

Let us mention two final points. It is not surprising that thanatopolitics was particularly manifest in so-called "revolutionary conservatism" (in Ernst Jünger, for example), namely, in a type of individualist, vitalist anarchism that prefigured Nazi thought.

What does the kamikaze act signify today? If we overlook the suffering and despair at the root of such a choice—absolutely political affects—we are again confronted with the suicidal reduction of the *Bios* to the *Zoe* which is enough to eliminate all biopolitical power *(puissance)* from the act itself (regardless of the judgment we can have on the latter).

There is a methodological approach to follow when speaking of biopolitics. Only by confronting the problem from a constitutive (genealogical) viewpoint will we be able to construct an efficient biopolitical discourse grounded in a series of apparatuses of subjective origin. We are well aware that the concept of "apparatus" *(dispositif)* as it appears in Foucault and Deleuze is understood by both philosophers as a group of homogeneous practices and strategies that define a state of power at a certain time. These are called apparatuses of control, or normative apparatuses. However, inasmuch as biopolitics is problematized in an ambiguous manner as the hold of power on life as well as the powerful and disproportionate reaction of life towards power, it seemed to us that the notion of apparatus should take on the same ambiguity. *An apparatus could just as well be the name for a strategy of resistance.*

When we speak of an "apparatus," we are referring to a type of genealogical thought whose development comprises the movements of desire and reasoning: we therefore subjectivate the power relations that pass through the world, society, institutional specificities, and individual practices.

This theoretical bent, shared by Foucault and Deleuze, is deeply anchored in the nonteleological philosophies that preceded *Historismus* or developed parallel to it. From Simmel to Benjamin, these philosophies led to theoretical formulations that enabled the ontological grid of culture and society to be reconstructed through the analysis of forms of life. Beyond our legitimate insistence on the origins of the concept of biopolitics in French poststructuralist thought, from this point of view it would be interesting to find a similar epistemological development in late nineteenth and early twentieth century German thought. Its fundamental figure would of course be Nietzsche. One should, in fact, analyze the whole Nietzschean effort to destroy positivist and vitalist teleology, and the way in which this same effort appears in the project of a genealogy of morals. The genealogy of morals is at the same time a collection of subjectivation processes and the space of a materialist teleology that take on the risk of projectuality, and recognize the finitude of their subjective source. It is what we have chosen to call, many years later and following in the footsteps of a Spinozan thought reinvested by the postmodern, a "disutopia."

We are now in a position to analyze biopolitics—and the resistance to it—as it appears, in the liberal and mercantile era, through its acquired functions upon leaving modernity, *within the framework of "real subsumption of society under capital."* When we speak of real subsumption of society under capital (capitalist development today), we are admittedly referring to the mercantilization of life, the disappearance of use value, the colonization of forms of life by capital, *as well as* to the construction of a resistance within this new horizon. Once again, one of the specificities of postmodernity is the *reversibility* of its effects: *any domination is also always resistance.* On this note, we should emphasize the surprising convergence of certain theoretical experiences at the heart of Western or postcolonial Marxism (we are of course thinking of so-called *Italian Workerism* [Operaismo], or certain branches of

Indian culturalism) with the philosophical positions of French poststructuralism. But we shall return to this.

We have already insisted on the importance of "real subsumption" understood as the essential phenomenon in the shift from the modern to the postmodern. However, the fundamental element of this transition also seems to be the *generalization of resistance* in each intersection of the great grid of real subsumption of society under capital. The discovery of resistance as a general phenomenon, a paradoxical opening in each link of power and a multiform apparatus of subjective production, is precisely where the postmodern affirmation lies.

Biopolitics is thus a contradictory context in/of life. By definition, it represents the extension of economic and political contradictions over the entire social fabric, but it also stands for the emergence of singularized resistances saturating it.

What do we mean exactly by "production of subjectivity?" We would like our analysis to go further than the anthropological dimension of the concept in Foucault and Deleuze. What is important, in this perspective, is the historical (and productive) concreteness of subjective constitution. The subject is productive; the production of subjectivity is therefore *a subjectivity that produces*. We will return to this definition in the following lectures, but we would like to emphasize that the cause or motor of this production of subjectivity is to be found inside power relations, in that complex game of relations that nevertheless remain constantly swept through by a desire for life. Inasmuch as this desire for life signifies the emergence of a resistance to power, resistance itself becomes the true motor of the production of subjectivity.

This definition of the production of subjectivity has been criticized for reintroducing a new dialectic of sorts: power includes resistance; resistance nourishes power. On another level, subjectivity is productive, just as the productivity of resistances constructs subjectivity. The argument is easily countered, however, if we return to the conception of resistance elaborated above: namely, the productive tie linking resistance to subjectivity and immediately characterizing singularities in their antagonism to biopower. It is unclear why alluding to antagonism should lead straight back to dialectics. If it is truly the singularity that acts, the relation to power that is established cannot lead to synthesis, overtaking, *Aufhebung*, in sum, to the Hegelian negation of negation. On the contrary, what we are dealing with is absolutely ateleological. Admittedly, singularities and resistances remain exposed to the risk and possibility of failure, *but the production of subjectivity always maintains the possibility, or better yet, the power* (puissance), *to emerge as an expression of excess.* This production cannot be reabsorbed into the heart of dialectical processes attempting to recompose the totality of the productive movement under transcendental form. Certain "reabsorption" effects are inevitable, of course, as certain particularly astute contemporary sociologists point out. But these are always random phenomena, spreading every which way, and never leading to foreseeable consequences. The machine of power, when it is forced to pass from the exercise of government to the practice of *governance*, proves itself incapable of running its own mechanical dimension in a unitary and necessary manner. Even if the reabsorption of subjective productions blocks new modes of life, this immediately leads to new resistances, new excess. This is from now on the only recognizable machine in the functioning of postmodern societies and politics: a machine, paradoxically, that can no longer be reduced to the mechanics of power.

It might be objected that politics, and state control, have always operated according to a type of logic within capitalism that attributed the unilateral negotiation and resolution of problems to relations of power. Power consists precisely in this. In the eighteenth century, theories of *Raison d'Etat* were not only arts of violence but also arts of mediation. When we transfer the theme of power into the context of biopolitical relations, we encounter—and this is novel—the exact opposite of this capacity for neutralization and immunization that we are being criticized for. It is the emergence of rupture that produces subjectivity; the intensity of excess is its mark.

Let us specify what we mean by the concept of excess, or, as we have called it elsewhere, the notion of measurelessness (*démesure*). The idea is born of a *new analysis of labor organization*, wherein value becomes the cognitive and immaterial product of creative action, and at the same time escapes the law of value (the latter understood in a strictly objective and economic manner). We encounter the same idea, on a different level, when we localize the *ontological dissymmetry* between how biopower functions and the potential *(puissance)* of biopolitical resistance. If power is measurable (measure and disparity *(écart)* are precious instruments of discipline and control), *potential* (puissance) *is, on the contrary, the non-measurable, the pure expression of irreducible differences.*

Finally, on a third level, we must be attentive to what is happening in theories of the state. Excess is always described as a production of power, and can take the form, for example, of a state of emergency. But this is an inconsistent, even grotesque, idea: a state of emergency can only be defined from within the indissoluble relation that links power to resistance. The power of the state is never absolute; that is how it *represents itself*, offering us a panorama of the absolute. It is always made up of a complex assemblage of relations that include resistance to it. It is not surprising that theories of dictatorship in Roman law—theories of the state of emergency—maintain that dictatorship can only develop during brief periods. As Machiavelli remarks, such temporal limitation does not refer to any guarantee of constitutionality but is used for efficiency. The state of emergency, even short-lived, is unacceptable for free minds, and can only be used as a last resort, in otherwise hopeless situations.

All theorizations of totalitarianism are just as grotesque, whether they stem from dictators themselves, or later, from certain figures of the contemporary political sciences, particularly during the cold war. They establish totalitarianism as a version of power that excludes all resistance. Though totalitarianism has existed—and its political practices still haunt our memory—the alleged "totality" of its power is a mystifying idea, and it is high time it is submitted to critique.

Let us return to the problem of the real dimensions of work, of its transformation during the passage from the modern to the post-modern, and of the interpretation—no doubt partial, albeit always reliable—of the production of subjectivity through the social activity of work. First of all, we would like to stress the importance of the convergence of Italian Workerist currents and poststructuralist French thought on the issue of the relation between the production of subjectivity and the transformation of labor regimes.

We have already alluded to the importance of the notion of "differences"—in the plural—and the centrality of its role in the thought and political practices that appeared in the strange "labora-tory" that was the Italy of the seventies. The convergence previously mentioned was patent not only in reference to the connection between subjectivation and material and/or immaterial productive forces, but also, and primarily, through the attempt to constitute an epistemology of the common on the base of singular differences. The convergence was therefore double; it concerned the link between labor and subjectivity as well as the one articulating singular differences and the common of singularities.

The mechanisms of the apparatus enabling the constitution of a true *materialist teleology of singularities* found support, at the juncture of these diverse theoretical formulations, in certain kinds of historiographical analyses (Italian Workerism for example). The latter affirmed the periodization and the historical definition of the caesura that had to be addressed theoretically and practically. In fact, Fordist organization of labor seemed to correspond to the disciplinarian organization of society; and, in the same way, the growing autonomous organization of cognitive labor today seems to correspond to organization by control. We should note in passing that when we speak of "materialist teleology" we never imply— contrary to all the transcendental teleologies and to all metaphysics of history—a predetermined *telos*, preexisting the material conditions of historical development. Rather, we are speaking of a *telos* that is permanently redefined, reformulated, reopened, and revived by social, political, economical, and—*last but not least*—historically antagonistic determinations. It seems clear that this is the only condition in which a philosophy of history can be both absolutely materialistic and totally immanent.

Of course, the convergence we are speaking of was not simply a Franco-Italian moment, but spread to numerous conceptual tendencies and investigative styles, in particular in the Anglo-Saxon world. On this point, we can cite certain Subaltern Studies already alluded to.

We must, however, insist on a fundamental element. There is a kind of *Marxian filigree* that runs through criticisms of the univocal conceptions of power, whether or not, paradoxically, they were produced under Marx's name. *Capitalist power*, as these critical currents maintain, *is always a relation*. Constant capital confronts variable capital; capitalist power confronts resistance from the labor force. This tension is what produces economic and historical development. It is true that "official" Marxism had confined the labor force and variable capital within relations objectively prefigured by economic laws. But certain Marxists, after 1968, started disintegrating this very prefiguration, which had been considered necessary and was closer to the Heideggerian conception of technology than to the proletarian desire for liberation. This is where the Workerism of the Italian laboratory of the seventies, Subaltern Studies, and the political analysis of power as formulated by Foucault and Deleuze all converge.

Let us go back to the relation between subjectivity and social work. We were saying that work possesses real new dimensions. The first remarkable aspect is no doubt the transformation of the dimension of temporality in the postmodern modification of productive structures. During Fordism, temporality was measured according to the law of value: an analytical, abstract, and quantitative temporality composed the productive value of capital through its opposition to the living time of labor. As Marx describes it, capitalist production represents the synthesis between the creativity of living work and the structures of exploitation organized by fixed capital and its temporal laws of productivity. In post-Fordism, on the contrary, temporality is neither simply nor totally enclosed within the structures of constant capital: as we have seen, intellectual, immaterial, and affective production (characterizing post-Fordist labor) reveals an excess. Abstract temporality, that is, the temporal *measure* of labor, cannot contain the creative energy of labor itself.

Within the new figure of the capitalist relation, excess enables the constitution of spaces of *self-valorization* that capital cannot entirely reabsorb. At best, these can only be recovered through a kind of permanent "wild chase" of this mass of autonomous labor, or, more precisely still, of this multitude of productive singularities. The constitution of capitalist temporality (that is, of the power of capital) can no longer be acquired or reconstructed dialectically. The production of merchandise is always followed by the production of subjectivities, which oppose each other as excess. This process takes the form of an apparatus that is virtually antagonistic and can counteract all capitalist synthesis. The Foucaldian distinctions between regimes of power and subjectivity are completely reinvested in this new reality of capitalist organization. They are represented by the scission between capitalist time/value and the singular valoriza-tion of the labor force. This is where the Spinozan opposition between power or *potestas* and potency or *potentia* (*puissance*) reemerges with great force.

Let us now return to an essential problem that we previously mentioned in passing: the measure of work and of capitalist time. If we consider that living work is the cause and constitutive motor (indifferently material or immaterial) of all forms of development, that the production of subjectivity is the fundamental key to escaping the dialectic of biopowers and, on the contrary, to constituting a biopolitical fabric, and that this production allows us to pass from a simple disciplinary regime to one that also contains the dimension of control at the same time as it allows the emergence of powerful and common insurgencies, then *the question of measure (the quan-tified rationality of valorization) becomes central.* It is paradoxically central, however, since the measures that capital sought to discipline and control are now elusive.

It will, no doubt, prove necessary to open a new field of research in order to determine whether the theme of measure can be proposed anew on the terrain of social production, according to new forms and modalities that will need to be defined. In that case, all analyses must presuppose the ontological break between living labor and constant capital. The fact is that the excess of living labor in relation to constant capital does not appear as an "immeasurable" production, "outside" quantitative measure. This is where the difficulty lies. It is rather a production that goes *beyond* the very idea of measure, that ceases to be defined as a negative overcoming of measurable limits to become, simply, in an absolutely affirmative and positive way, the *potential* (puissance) of living labor. And it then becomes legitimate to consider, at least as a tendency, the end of exploitation. And this is no doubt what Foucault and Deleuze refer to when speaking of processes of subjectivation.

We have now arrived before a new definition of *capital as crisis*. From the point of view of constant capital, such a capitalist relation seems completely parasitical. We have also arrived where antagonisms that involve the production of subjectivity and the expression of living work might be recomposed. In the following sessions, we shall explore how a new theorization of the crisis of capital has become necessary.

We started out by trying to circumscribe the notions of biopower, biopolitics, discipline, and control. We must now address the notion of multitude. In fact, the entire analysis we are developing is meant to constitute the presupposition of that notion. As a provisional point of reference to be further elaborated and modified, let us propose the following definition. The concept of multitude follows from the relation between a constitutive form (of singularity, of invention, of risk, to which the entire transformation of labor and the new measure of temporality lead) and a practice of power (the destructive tendency of labor-value that capital must today enforce). But while capital used to be able to reduce the multiplicity of singularities to something organic and unitary (a class, a people, a mass, a collection), this process no longer functions. *The multitude must necessarily be thought of as a nonorganic, differential, and powerful* (puissante) *multiplicity.*

Workshop 3

Between Globalization and Exodus:

Peace and War

In the preceding lectures, particularly in the second, we attempted to define the concepts of biopower, biopolitics, control, and discipline, and began approaching that of multitude. While we are able to clarify these notions, other concepts forged by modern thought have either been progressively diluted, have become hazy, or have completely stopped functioning (the notion of "people," "nation" or "class," for example). We contend that the idea of sovereignty must be submitted to an increasing critique.

When we confront the reality of globalization, the crisis and transformation of the political concepts of modern thought undergo an impressive acceleration. Once the modern notions of temporality and measure, linked to an old understanding of work and social order, weaken, then all the other concepts disappear in batches. *Globalization radically blasts away the set of old criteria of measure.* And since the latter are not only linked to spatial dimensions but also to temporal assemblages, this triggers a whole sequence of conceptual dissolutions.

In this third lecture, as you will have understood, we will address the transformation of the political concepts of modernity, taking stock of the *irreversible character* of the globalization process in the productive, political, institutional, and cultural dimensions of post-modernity. By irreversibility, we mean, first of all, the objective impossibility of reinstating the panorama and the conditions of Fordist production and of the Keynesian market. These were at the base of modernity, and cannot be recovered. In this respect, we must speak of an ontological caesura, and build from there. Secondly, this irreversibility applies to the modification of subjective behavior both in terms of labor and from the point of view of the constitution of the social tie. But we shall return to this question. Thirdly, globalization represents the destruction of the spatial determinations of the modern state. Globalization brings about the irreversibility of the crisis of the nation-state and of the related concepts of people and sovereignty. The entire modern history of political thought, affirmed as hegemonic, tips over. Even the "alternative" history within modernity, from Machiavelli to Spinoza, is similarly shaken, and becomes increasingly difficult to use in a positive manner. The only way to utilize this kind of "alternative" tradition is to bring it to *a radical level of ontological alterity*, which we believe is possible.

The fundamental concepts of the political field must be modified and reformulated in view of this ontological alterity. Let us recall Jacques Derrida's emphasis on the necessity of deconstructing the conceptual tools of the great metaphysics of the Western world. We again invoke the ontological intensity of the crisis at hand. It interrupts an entire classical tradition ceaselessly upheld by Christianity and then by modern thought, affirming the essential union of the concepts of *origin* and *command* in the concept of principle (*archè*). However, the modification of state processes and modern conceptual tools is neither limited to the meaning of the notions implied therein, nor to the form and dimension of their mode of reasoning.

This modification concerns ontological reality itself, and illustrates its decisive transformation.

The discussion of the concept of measure is therefore essential. It concerns the measure of productive value, namely, the problem of the validity of the Marxian, in reality classical, law (from Smith to Ricardo) of the time/value relation. This law clearly does not hold, meaning that the real measuring function of labor and development is inapplicable. However, the crisis of this law, and the subsequent questioning of the concept of measure force the figures, apparatuses, and articulations of the social determinations of modernity to redefine themselves as a *biopolitical regime*. More generally, production and culture must revise their evaluation criteria as established by the old categories of modernity. *A mobile and flexible world rises before us:* when we look back at the history of our societies, first the immutable rhythm of working the earth, then the regular repetition of Taylorized time and of the industrial massification of the metropolis, *what difference do we discover today? What irreducible distance with the past must we describe and understand?*

If we interpret globalization as a biopolitical event, we must acknowledge the importance of its effects, and the strength of its efficiency as an *apparatus of subordination*. Whereas in the seventeenth century, the origin of modern political thought is (national) society, we must now think according to global society. Whereas we find functional rationality at the base of modern political thought, from within a global society, we must now think with the criteria of biopolitical reason and according to the norms of biopowers. Speaking of the criteria of biopolitical reason, we invoke a kind of knowledge that might immediately determine the synthesis of reason and affect, truth and communication. Speaking of norms and of biopowers, we mean the attempt to radically control this biopolitical reason and life in general. Despite the contradictions, divergences, and drifts that we can easily ascertain, *we must emphasize that the relation between biopolitical apparatuses and norms of biopowers definitively displaces all the dimensions of knowledge and ethics.*

Let us therefore, from the point of view of globalization, start to enquire about how the political categories of the modern have changed, not according to the effects of the transformation brought on by the workers' struggle in the Western world, but according to other players, more peripheral although no less important. These are the proletarians of what has been called the Third World, individuals subjected to the rules of colonialism and imperialism in the nineteenth and twentieth centuries. We all have in mind examples from Brazil, South Africa, India, China, or Iran. Although these differ greatly, historically and socially, they do possess an important common element. Indeed, their underdevelopment was constructed according to the imperialist functions defined in classical theories, yet a network of colonial, racial, and religious biopowers was added, making the rules of the central power more complex. Mercantile exports and the accumulation of absolute surplus value do not define imperialism as much as *the permanence of biopowers that have become consubstantial with the very functioning of colonial and imperialist rules.* It was on this terrain that the functional rationality of imperialism played its adventure of conquest in a rising fury.

But beneath this power, we must also perceive the drive towards "something else": an entire history of resistances, insurrectional movements, experimentations in cooperation and alternative solidarity, attempts at political and cultural autonomy, struggles, and utopian projects of liberation. In colonized countries more than anywhere else, *the presence of ramified biopowers to an antagonism just as diffuse and powerful has been impressive.*

If we choose to consider events through this viewpoint, we will note a strong homogeneity of local situations of resistance and struggle that try to define development in terms of "*another*" *modernity*. It is probably for this reason that those populations freed from the yoke of colonialism are outraged by the reactionary attempts to present colonialism under the guise of an alleged "beneficial" benevolence.

When we refer to "another" modernity, we are pointing to another way towards certain economic, social, and political levels of *welfare* and freedom than the one motioned to by the West. More precisely, we wish to emphasize how the forces and dynamics this alterity proposes can be used to create models of autonomous development based on different values. If we do not analyze the phenomenon of underdevelopment in this perspective, we incur the risk of losing the meaning of that great adventure of anticolonial resistance and of the network of illusions and forces that contributed to it. In certain cases such illusions were nefarious; they were also sometimes very powerful, and almost always revolutionary. Even the "socialist revolution" (Russia, China, Cuba) encountered figures and meanings in the Third World that completely transformed the linearity of capitalist modernity. Although it is completely natural that capitalist rationality condemned these attempts, one cannot but recognize the exalting character of this project for an alternative modernity, and the strength with which it tried to impose itself.

Perhaps the polemical spirit in which we consider the analyses labeling the contemporary period *hypermodern* rather than postmodern will now be better understood. There is, in fact, a model in the idea of hypermodernity—we do not know whether it is

Heideggerian, or socialist—that affirms that the technology and form of modern development cannot be overcome. This model, while paradoxically affirming its historical continuity in relation to that against which it defines itself, stands against the possibility of instituting other values and other paradigms. *Now the rupture between modernity and what follows is not only temporal but also substantial.* It concerns the very contents of development, their value, and more generally the intensity of subjective apparatuses. Thus "alterity," for example, is not the opposition between development and underdevelopment, but between underdevelopment and *another* development. We must again insist on the depth of the historical caesura with which we started these lectures. Indeed, we are reading the succession of two historical and political moments, and their corresponding theorizations, yet alterity is already undeniably present at the heart of modernity, once the permanence and opposition of two lines are identified: the absolutist one, following Hobbes, and the democratic one, espousing Spinoza. Today, of course, inside the postmodern, this internal alternative does not have the exact signification it did three centuries ago. But we must analyze its power (*puissance*).

In all of the countries alluded to above, the debate seemed to have crystallized historically around certain important precepts (*mots-d'ordre*): no to homogenization, cultural and political subordination, economic underdevelopment; yes, on the other hand, to a path towards freedom and autonomy. The entire first period of anticolonial revolutions was constructed on such projects. A second phase followed the victory and hegemony of these projects for independence after the Bandung Conference, with the diminished importance of colonial processes in the workings of state governments and the rise of movements of national liberation. This second moment was characterized by a kind of *peripheral Fordism*, and despite often fierce negotiations, by reduced yet still acute dependence: brutally stated, a *neocolonial phase*. Indeed, viewed from the "center," the situation at the "peripheries" of the colonial empire was relatively clear: anticolonial and antiimperialist struggles had blasted away the direct axes of power previously representing the power of the "central" countries. The latter could only count on reorganizing their power in terms of development. This development in dependence had to articulate market elements with residue of the colonial question. The possibility of integration through development was allowed, yet it had to function within the schemas of constraint and domination established by the "central" countries. *Dependency became hierarchical structuring.* Thus, paradoxically, the definitive anticolonial victories coincided with the triumph of peripheral Fordism.

This phase, that characterizes the second half of the twentieth century for the most part, can be *assessed* today as one of reproduced and hierarchically organized "dependency." But through globalization, it also constitutes the condition for a definitive rupture with the presuppositions above. If we look at development in its diachronic (historical) dimension, globalization imposes *a passage from dependence to interdependence*, and revives instances of autonomy and powers of development in a completely different context. This process is extremely ambiguous and complex, but it always comprises other—definitive?—attacks against the measures and rules of economic dependency.

When considering this series of phenomena, we must return to the hypothesis—central to this seminar—according to which it is necessary to emphasize *the crises of all the laws and forms of measure of capitalist development.* At stake is not simply the crisis of the law of value, and of the relations developing between the working class and the state in advanced capitalist countries. We must also grasp the quality of this crisis, often interpreted according to alternatives proposed by Third World countries, and during anticolonial revolutions. Enlightenment reason was crushed beneath the weight of a close link to the development of capitalism and burdened by accumulation founded on exploitation. Today, this stands opposed to a biopolitical reason linking development to reclaiming and reaffirming community values, extra-European forms of civilization, or those desires not yet subjected to Western consumerist monopoly. We must be careful, however: this opposition, this alternative to capitalist development will inevitably affect the West itself. Globalization reveals the limits of imperialist action on the part of nation-states; work and production are becoming social and claiming the fundamental elements of life, needs, and desires. Historically speaking, we find ourselves perhaps today at the heart of the transformation and homogenization of the crises of the law of value, and of capitalist enlightenment reason.

The crux of our discussion lies in this idea of the crisis of measure, or, more precisely, the idea of the possibility for capital and its elites to measure development. The concepts we have expounded until now—globalization, development, modernity and "another" modernity, dependence and interdependence—place us at the heart of postmodernism. But this transformation is also an explosion, the sign of a basic mutation, a paradigmatic shift. The crisis of the idea of meaning has qualitative, irreversible, and enormously important effects that imply the impossibility of ascribing a stable and complete figure to processes of government on the field of globalization. It is in this crisis of measure, control, and govern-ment that tendency towards Empire, namely the constant push towards global government, also enters a state of crisis.

In this situation, war seems the only possible solution. *Pax belli*: peace is only possible through war. *With the disappearance of the internal criteria that allow the self-regulation and the self-valorization of development, it is the violence of the strongest that creates the norm.* The idea of the market essentially implies the hypothesis of a society dominated by binding reason. Violence is just its complement; it guarantees the smooth running of society and widens the terms of the market. When the market, when criteria for production and accumulation sweep through the entire social field, when norms of social regulation and measure enter into crisis, when alternative criteria for valorization appear in both central and peripheral fields of capitalism, then the only solution for the systemic forces with the power to dominate capitalism is to recognize irrationality: *the universal declaration of a state of emergency.* The situation in which we live is characterized by such a "state of emergency." Contrary to what fascist theories maintain, this state of emergency is not the urgency of power, in fact quite understandable, when faced with disorder. On the contrary, it is the vehement attempt to reintro-duce old criteria of measure based neither on the productivity of systems, the participation of subjects nor the articulation of inter-dependencies, but simply on the maintenance of privileges and the reproduction of established power. A police force exercising on a global scale replaces the normalizing character of productive structures and the functional character of their hierarchy (whether the latter was a mystification is not important: it was, in fact, an efficient one). *In this transition towards the postmodern, the bellicose structures of the modern period are transformed into central-ized police structures; armies become bands of soldiers and mercenary troops.* And since police activities— *Polizeiwissenschaft*—now occur within a *biopolitical fabric*—as we have seen—this new war takes the form of a war *that creates order.* It builds nations, contracts certain charitable organizations or NGOs, and provides itself with general-ized instruments of control wherever weaknesses appear in social organization or in economic development. With Michael Hardt, we argued this point at length in *Multitude*, and I will not linger upon it. What I wish to emphasize, however, is that these solutions to problems of development and these dynamics of domination, based on the complete absence of a shared project, operate within precise historical dimensions. I also wish to emphasize that a new order cannot be constructed from these repressive techniques. The latter must therefore continually—and inexorably—sustain expressions of resistance, revolt, as well as civic, and moral refusal.

What interests us above all is the emergence of an ordering function of war after the disappearance of measuring or regulatory criteria. We strongly disagree with those who believe that postmodern sovereignty—including its bellicose variant—only develops in a repressive manner. *For the most part, such conceptions overestimate biopower while underestimating the possibility of resistance.* Reactionary thought insists on the "Auschwitz model" in order to cynically trans-form it into an example of the invincible character of power: often stating its horror, it implicitly exalts its irresistible power. Reactionary thought refuses to consider resistance as an invincible ontological process, yet Guernica or Fallujah are living proof.

War has always pretended to have an ordering finality in post-modern capitalism, even when it acknowledges the enormous corruption of the productive process and of its military management. Ontologically, resistance immediately denies that claim. Modernity's order can no longer suppress postmodern disorder; Hobbes crumbles before Guernica and Fallujah.

So the question now is: what is the new order implied by this function of imperial war? It entails the security of privacy, of the market, of global commerce, and the maintenance of hierarchies of dependence and/or of central rules of interdependence. The structure of command exerts a hypertrophic pressure on these juridical elements and on their policing. This coercion corresponds to another hypertrophy: the illusion of the self-organization of the market. Power believes that autonomous market organization—that is, the capacity of the *lex mercatoria*, the norms laid down by the multinationals, to give rise to a new global order—can come to frame its own project. Not only is this unverifiable, it is false. In the following lecture, we shall consider the critical relation between the public, the private, and the common spheres in the new organization of the market. Formally, however, we must now insist on the juridical and political effects this new bellicose order is trying to impose.

This new order presents itself as:

1. The dissolution/disappearance of borders;
2. The end/exhaustion of international law;
3. The need to dominate a *beyond*.

If we follow the capitalist claim to the establishment of a new order, and limit ourselves to a critical and formal reading of the conceptual redefinition this implies, certain preliminary problems arise:

a. A series of problems linked to *the dissolution/disappearance of borders*, and consequently, *to the eclipse of the concepts of nationhood and people from the political debate*. How can we interpret these processes? What are the real tensions crisscrossing, dissolving and recomposing these borderless spaces? There are generally two points of view on the issue. According to the language of power, one must intervene on the mobility brought about by the effacement of national borders through governmental practices that can weigh upon productive processes and articulations, population transfers, and the biopolitical dynamics of innovation. Governments must determine hierarchies and exclusions in order to maintain the values and measures of their domination. From the point of view of freedom, on the contrary, migrations, miscegenation, integration, the mixing of populations, etc., represent the very matter of the unstoppable process of the crumbling of borders.

b. The necessity to address the issue of the end of Westphalien type international law. There is no need to review the entire history of international law; we must simply remember its contractual nature, meaning that it is a contract between subjects and a nation. The U.N. is the ultimate result of this process. Yet the crisis of the United Nations paradigmatically represents the very limits of this contractual process. *How can we imagine a beyond of the U.N.?* What kind of new regulatory mechanism can we invent that would span the phenomenon of globalization? Clearly, the strength of globalization requires global management—at least in terms of *extension*—juggling development and underdevelopment, dependence and interdependence, unity and articulations. Globalization must also be governed in terms of *intensity*, at biopolitical and sociopolitical levels. The exercise of international power necessarily goes hand in hand with more and more intense processes of *governance*. The third problem of political representation remains open: how to organize political representation on a global scale?

When we address these questions, we are not confusing the issues concerning forces of domination with those flowing through forces of subversion. Sometimes, however, they become superimposed. This marks a terrain of struggle, and implies that protagonists' positions are informed by completely divergent points of view. Such is the case for the argument, often put forward in Europe, that the nation-state cannot be surpassed, as it is the only way to identify a space of power in which to act, and to transform capitalism. Not only is that a false affirmation from the point of view of the transformations of international organizations and of global order, it is also profoundly reactionary. *The nation-state finds its place within the global network of biopowers; it belongs to those world masters that control both the knots and grid of the network.*

c. What does it mean to go *beyond* these issues? This brings us back to the theme of measure, to an "outside" (*hors mesure*) and a "beyond" (*au delà de la mesure*) of measure. Clearly, one cannot reduce the latter to a simple immeasurable, outside of measure. We must reason with a new kind of subjectivity that finds its place exactly between the two, nestled between the *outside* (dehors) and the *beyond*. For this, we must bet on the excess of immaterial labor, on the irreducibility of this new power (*puissance*) in regards to the modern critique of political economy and politics. But foremost, we link our critical insistence on the new power (*puissance*) of labor to the hypothesis/reality affirming and developing an "alter-modernity." By this we mean the power within political, civic, and subversive movements, although they remain exposed to the danger of recuperation by the global order, to build towards a new biopolitical reason. Acknowledging the "outside" (*dehors*) of measure and the excess of common productive power is (or *should* be) a means to produce a new horizon for life, a new conception of the human. In fact, the *outside* has disappeared; there is just the *beyond*. Even the *other* appears under its guise. Immaterial/cognitive productive time is a time of excess: it is a constitutive time within the relation to the other. There are innumerable voices protesting in the name of the *other*, brandishing its concrete, nonconceptual existence. Even this *other*, previously rejected from the unitary order of command, or included by subjection or slavery, belongs within the new paradigm, inserted into the process alongside the productive central forces of the globalized world. This is a difficult passage to grasp. We are living a transitional period, and the change is not instantaneous. Concepts dilute into time, into this material temporality, this ceaselessly revived activity that forms and affirms them.

In this third lecture, we have insisted on such concepts as *peace, war, state of emergency, resistance*. We lingered on the notions of *borders, people, nation*, and more implicitly perhaps, of *exodus, emancipation*, and *liberation*. Let us keep this conceptual toolbox close at hand, and open to examination.

Beyond Private and Public: the Common

In the previous lectures, we invoked the following historical, political, categorial, and diachronic themes: the caesura between the modern and the postmodern, the biopolitical figure of reason—and an adequate construct of the concept of biopolitics—the global dimension in which to situate political discussion, and finally, the emergence of new antagonisms, with *the concept of multitude cohering the multiple resistances that singularities produce*. We also evoked a certain number of fundamental theoretical issues: the crisis of the rational criteria orienting capitalist development crystallized around the measure of work, but consequently, also the "outside" and "beyond" of capitalism, *exodus and multitude*. In this fourth lecture, we would like to start from the base, namely, consider the categories, previously approached with diachronic parameters, according to their subjective genesis. This will thus be a synchronic approach, in which we shall consider the action of the singularities that form the multitude.

Two essential objections are generally leveled against the concept of multitude. The first denounces its incapacity to present itself as an *antisystemic power*. The second objects that *the passage from the in-itself to the for-itself of the multitude* cannot be described, and that the multitude cannot be defined as an instance of unitary recomposition liable to develop efficient political action without dialectical mystification.

The first objection, formulated primarily by Etienne Balibar, cannot be countered without taking into account the insufficiency of its demand. For Immanuel Wallerstein and those who refer to his work, an "antisystemic" movement signified a movement opposed to capitalist exploitation in "central" countries as well as to imperialist structures in Third World countries. Such a movement was structurally able to orient itself antagonistically according to imperialist politics. The term provided a unitary framework of reference, in which the working class remained an absolute postulate associating class and antiimperialist struggles.

Today, however, the term has lost its import, mostly due to the reduced difference between First and Third Worlds. It has also become increasingly banal: all anticapitalist movements, even the peripherally hegemonic, appear as antisystemic. The problem remains of defining the multitude in terms other than those of the traditional discourse on class struggle, terms that might relay the drive of global subversion in the age of Empire. In "antisystemic" thought, the scope of the class struggle was in reality greatly reduced in favor of Third-Worldism. Synthesis only occurred on a superior, completely ideological level, according to a classical deterministic conception of the development of struggles and of capitalism itself: the predetermination of crisis, the tendency towards falling rates of profit, etc. What could antisystemic still mean to a realist conception of the class struggle? How could a thinker such as Balibar (who, in fact, represents a number of critical positions towards America and Europe) fall prey to nostalgia for traditional determinism as proposed by dialectical materialism? It is true that the objectively anticapitalist definition of the multitude cannot be reduced to its conceptual dimension. The multitude is not simply a concept: it is a new reality. And we cannot determine whether it is anticapitalist by analyzing its concept, but by observing its movement. This question brings us back to the second objection mentioned above.

This second objection carries more weight, and, in fact, it repeats the first. Pierre Macherey articulated it, among others. Beyond the fundamental issue of the passage from the in-itself to the for-itself—under whose apparently tragic character lays an unwittingly comic side—the problem is to understand how the multitude connects to a unit of action. And, if this is possible, how it is antagonistic. We propose the following answer: *the emergence of the common* (from a productive and political point of view) *at the heart of the multitude is what makes it subjectively efficient and objectively antagonistic*. This means, from the point of view of production, that the common represents the condition of all social valorization. From the political point of view, it is the very form of the organization of subjectivity. We are not looking here to affirm a unit of action, but to show the coherence of an assemblage (*agencement*) at work.

In order to define the common from the point of view of production, we must insist on the following: when we consider the multitude as a labor force, we grasp it according to a new, common homogeneity of the productive fabric, and to the acknowledgement of its powers of transformation. There is a common material fabric, a glitch in ontological constitution through which immaterial, cognitive, and cooperative production is organized by processes of valorization, and strongly harnesses other forms of production. It would be easy to show that almost all forms of organization of the labor of productive sectors, including those previously excluded from the framework of communication and the information society, are now subsumed within a global unity sharing the same specificities of exploitation.

The real subsumption of labor under capital finds its strongest expression here. In agriculture for example, more and more complex and sophisticated computational models are set to work—from seed analyses to weather forecasting. What used to be considered traditional forms of female labor (domestic and emotional labor, healing, etc.) are integrated into the general system of labor organization, and even establish a marked raise in productivity. Beyond the broadening of labor to include what had previously been excluded from it, the barycenter of valorization has shifted towards activities previously considered unproductive. We can thus speak of a *becoming-woman of labor*, understood not only as the feminization of labor in general, but also as the redefinition of spaces of valorization. Finally, to limit ourselves to a last example, the economy and the organization of labor in the service industry imply a growing hegemony of immaterial labor that, in reality, irreversibly applies to the entire scenario of production.

Yet wherever we find exploitation, we always encounter resistance, antagonism.

It is therefore not surprising that some demands for a minimum salary, a citizenship income, appear under the guise of a reflection both on this common hegemony of social production and on the valuing of the singular content that each working subject brings to this production. From this point of view, the socialization of capitalist accumulation can only be considered as the material basis that enables claims for a relative equality of income. Inasmuch as all work, whether material or immaterial, is indispensable and is always subsumed and articulated within the capitalist domination of society, there is no reason to distinguish and to assume a hierarchy between forms of salary.

The common provides a base for revealing those dimensions of immaterial and cooperative work that have been rendered objectively homogeneous. Yet it is also, most importantly, *a continuous power* (puissance) *and production, a capacity for transformation and cooperation.* The multitude can thus be defined as the jointing of an objective base (the common as a base for accumulation, constituted by material and immaterial forces) with a subjective one (the common as production, along a retreating border and ever renewed values; the common as the result of processes of subjectivation). The relations between the dimensions of production (of investment) and the dimensions of work (and/or consumption)—according to the classical conception formulated in the economic table from Quesnay to Marx—have clearly become unstable. Balance can only be obtained through permanent compromise and renewed adaptation. We find ourselves as in the presence of a doubling of forces, rather than before a unified capitalist front of command. The objective and unitary figure of capitalism's process of production and accumulation has markedly weakened and no doubt definitively changed. It opens onto a new expression of subjectivity, one more independent and autonomous, which can construct antagonistic forms from within the very process of production to give rise to the invention of a *common*.

Here, we believe a brief recapitulation of Marx's description of the concept of capital is in order, both to distance ourselves from it as well as to renew it. Marx divides the concept of capital into "constant capital" (C) and "variable capital" (V). C, which Marx also defines as "total capital," presents itself both as "fixed capital" (the totality of the means of production) and "circulating capital" (the totality of the means of the circulation of goods). Today, however, the organization of capital has altered. What has essentially changed is V, the totality of the labor force. First of all, today's labor force has incorporated certain elements of fixed capital (in other words, it carries with it certain means of production, in the brain: properties that have not been constructed by C, that do not belong to the total process of capital, but exist in relative autonomy). When speaking of cognitive work, we are speaking of this new faculty of the work force: *the means of production has become internal to the singularities engaged in the organization of labor.*

Secondly, if the labor force has internalized elements of fixed capital, variable capital will henceforth be able to circulate independently, inasmuch as its autonomy in regards to constant capital allows for its independence. If all this is phenomenologically verifiable, we should arrive at the conclusion that constant (and/or total) capital can no longer contain the labor force (and subordinate it exclusively). Marx's concept of capital was unitary, or better yet, it was a dialectical synthesis of fixed and variable capital. This synthesis no longer occurs. *Variable capital—the labor force—has acquired a certain autonomy.* The cycle of constant capital is henceforth characterized as a contradictory and insoluble relation between capital and the work force. Their synthesis can only occur superficially, in an ontic dimension, since the labor force (V) has found, ontologically, a space of autonomy.

All this leads us to define the common, essentially, as the open field in which living labor (the labor force, V) moves independently. It is the terrain where the results of the production of independent subjectivities and the cooperation of singularities is accumulated and consolidated. *The common is the sum of everything that the labor force (V) produces independently of C (constant capital, total capital) and against it.*

From this point of view, it is clear that the common is neither some sort of "organic depth," nor something physically determinable. According to us, it corresponds to the new expression of a contradictory relation between antagonistic subjects. Dialectical reabsorption is no longer possible, nor is linear subsumption: instead, the contradictory quality of the relation exalts singularities as differences and jars the formation of unifying criteria.

This leads to a new form of expression of subjectivities. From this perspective, the second objection raised against the concept of multitude—the impossibility of connecting it to a unity of action—seems quite inconsistent. *The multitude's unity of action is the multiplicity of expressions it is capable of.* If we consider the question from the political point of view rather than from the economic one (as in analyses of labor, accumulation, and exploitation), this ramified difference in the action of the multitude expresses a difference of desires, of subjective *claims*, that has nothing to do with the unity of a process of command (henceforth rather juridical than economic). At issue is the continuity of antagonistic expressions, with all the richness and diversity that implies. Seen from this perspective, the sovereign unity of the state suddenly appears "emptied," as does the unifying discipline of the expressions of labor. If we can one day speak of unity—juridically and in terms of capitalist accumulation—it will be because we shall have transformed unity into a relation between variables, a community of singularities. *The common is an activity, not a result; it is an assemblage* (agencement) *or an open continuity, not a densification of control.*

Having established this effective dimension of the common, we can examine the critique of the notions of public and private as transmitted by the juridical and political tradition.

Capitalist appropriation is always private, even (and especially) when the contractual form of appropriation is not only private but also public. *How could what is private and capitalist live without the overdetermination of what is public and state controlled?* In bourgeois culture, the construction of law is nothing but the construction of formally universal norms allowing for private appropriation. It does not seem useful to recall Marx's now classic pages on Hegel's *Philosophy of Right*, nor to speak of the wonderful advances made on those grounds by the contemporary critiques of public and private law within communist culture, from Pashukanis to Poulantzas. If something remains to be studied in traditional Marxism, it is this critical effort, this destructive penetration that the science of reversal has exerted against the universal categories of private and public bourgeois law.

Passing from private to public appropriation through the state, the categories of appropriation themselves do not change. Public law arises from the transformation of juridical institutions—in the passage from feudal and patrimonial state appropriation to bourgeois and advanced capitalist state development. It can even go so far as to be organized as planning (indifferently capitalist or socialist). In the modern state, there is no real difference between private and public appropriation: both are based on rules of exploitation and exclusion, on rules that are, and will remain, fundamental to the management of capital.

The greatest paradox appears when subjective rights themselves are qualified as "public subjective rights." This means that bourgeois law can only accept subjective rights (corresponding to singular *claims*) if they have previously been made public, conceded to individuals by the authority of the state, prefigured and defined by it. The figure of the modern state is based on this complex absorption of productive subjectivity in a concept of command that is the immediate corollary to the practice of exploitation.

Today however, things are different. With the passage into the postmodern, and with the difficult survival of the traditional categories of law, the relation of these categories with reality is dissolving. The division between public and private law, and between private and public appropriation, is evidently in crisis. We must not only consider the multiplication of processes of privatization, or those processes of administrative assimilation of public law into private law that have become the general principle of *governance* activity. The point is not really to formulate a sophisticated critique of these processes. In reality, public and private spheres are henceforth indistinct. Their distinction is only maintained in the so-called "science of law," that is, on the field of practices of domination. The drastic referential shift comes, sometimes in an unclear and slightly mystified way, with the revelation, *the emergence of the common*. We could provide numerous examples of the indistinction between private and public at the heart of which the common emerges. This is particularly visible in those domains modified by the development of recent technologies. What happens on the web, and the way in which public and private rights enter into conflict with common practices, is now a daily phenomenon. What is happening with biotechnologies is of the same order, perhaps with even greater intensity. The products of these technologies, and their common, natural base, cannot be separated by private operations. No mediation remains between capitalist appropriation (and the technological structures that correspond to it) and the instances of the singular emergence of living work, or those actions of the multitude with a strong effect on technologies themselves. Capitalist command no longer appears as a preconstituted and functional structure for private exploitation and appropriation. In this context, capital attempts, *a posteriori*, to grasp the direct, immediate, and expressive activity of subjects. The capitalist exploitation of telematics and life technologies has thus become absolutely parasitical, in principle and in practice. We cannot think of the web, or of biotechnological networks, without direct subjective participation. As for capital, the question is neither to elucidate nor to circumvent the division between public and private, but simply to take advantage of the common—understood, as we have seen, as *common activity*.

In late modernity, the philosophical perception of the crisis between public and private was far ranging, as was the confusion to which it led.

In the 1970s, Habermas, by constructing the category of "public space" and articulating it upon the subjectivity of "public opinion," attempted to reformulate the relation between the public and the private in a transcendental manner, strongly emphasizing their interaction. Habermas thus attributed a transcendental definition to the common, which could be articulated (and even dismembered) in its functional applications. On this point, we reach the limits—or the most direct presuppositions—of German hypermodern thought.

In the United States, what has been called the "communitarian" school (from Taylor to Sanders) considerably developed the theme of the "common," although its definition was built upon organic references. In reality, it transfigured and anchored public tendencies internal to the *welfare state*. This transfiguration often grew sterile with its emphasis on legally organizing systems of social rights (that are almost naturalistic); when it did not, it always relied on transcendental or dialectic contents. From this point of view, it is not surprising that Taylor (like Habermas himself) constructs his concept of "public space" by reinterpreting the concept of "interaction" taken from the genesis of the Hegelian dialectic.

Our conception of the common, on the contrary, refutes all the supposed original divisions between public and private, as well as their successive reformulations. The multitude is a collection of singularities, a cooperative fabric that links together infinite singular activities. *It is on such terrain that we must openly reconstruct—or better yet, elaborate—the concept of the common.*

Is a juridical definition of the common possible?

Let us take an example. We shall start from the definition of public service as given in "public law." In this perspective, public service is understood as part of the spread of state law and public guarantees on the social life of individuals. Public service is thus part of biopower, and as such, its funding, once the welfare state begins, relies on the dynamics of deferred salary, thus implying that the means of private appropriation of living work are transferred to state control and guaranteed by state authority.

However, according to our conception of the common, there is a new definition of public service that can reverse the relation we have just described. The move is no longer from the monopoly of specific natural resources to the development of the community of services, from the expansion of state rights to the functional control of citizens. Rather, the shift now occurs from *the increase and accumulation of the singular claims of the multitude to the idea and practice of a common service.* Public service, or better yet, common service, must become the condition of common life, and consequently, of the expansion of singularities. In France, the struggles that took place in 1995–1996 against the reform of retirement laws brought to light a common dimension in which all citizens took part, beyond the union led labor corps dimension of resistance movements. Still in France, the independent cultural workers' struggle (*les intermittents du spectacle*), ongoing since 2000, has elaborated a new conception of public service as establishing and developing the activities of the common. The right to public service is not something *the state grants its citizens.* Rather, it is something that is *socially and politically demanded by immaterial and cognitive work,* and by the cooperative capacity such work necessarily implies. Public service is the condition of common possibility under which the power of labor can be expressed, inasmuch as the power of labor has become common: public service exposes a power that is already realized and that no state can claim to destroy.

When we consider the accumulation realized through the cooperative networks of singularity, public service represents a common structure. The clearest indication of this is the demand for a universal citizenship income, thus acknowledging that the common lies at the base of all production.

Bourgeois law considers the public domain as an extension of the private one; socialism makes the same claim. Both socialist reformism (the idea that a continuous development of public rights would modify the relations of private production) and the socialist idea of revolution (the construction of public conditions for social reproduction through the takeover of power) rest beneath the blanket capitalism has provided. Public law always presents itself as an expression of biopower. Inversely, *the law of the common is always a biopolitical expression of the multitude.*

Let us insist on the following: the common—its demands, its acknowledgment and its politics—does not constitute a "third way" that might mediate between private and public. Rather, it is a "second way," *antagonistic* and *alternative* in regards to the management of capital and to the effects that capital (the private and/or public property of the means of production) can have on common life and on the desires that are expressed there. The law of the common can only be conceived along with the destruction of exploitation—private or public—and the radical democratization of production.

A small digression might be useful here. Let us inquire as to the status of the financialization of the economy, in the context of this crisis affecting the classic division between the public and the private—and paradoxically, opening onto the constitution of a new horizon of the common. There are two opposing stances on the question. The first considers financialization as the linear and/or dialectical expansion of private capitalist production. The second, on the contrary, refers it back to the representation of a common production, that becomes, by that means, somehow mystified. According to this second interpretation, cognitive work cannot find other means of accumulation (and of representation) than those belonging to financialization processes.

The second hypothesis seems the less erroneous of the two. The Marxist tradition provides us with several similar cases: the moment of the "formal subsumption" of labor, in the first period of capitalist development, thus corresponded to the development of joint stock companies—what Marx defined as a "socialism of capital." Clearly, the extended industrialization of contemporary capitalism would never have been possible without the construction of banking capital and the activity of joint stock companies. Such companies are produced as industrial organization unifies the subordination of labor. They represent the condition of development of industrial organization. *Does today's financialization constitute a kind of "communism of capital,"*—to keep the Marxist image. Is it the privileged interpreter of the birth and expansion of the multitude, as well as its most formidable adversary? Is financialization the way capitalism understands how the system of production is transformed by cognitive and immaterial labor? Is it the technological instrument used to cancel all possibilities of accumulation of the revolutionary potential *(puissance)* of cognitive labor and/or all possibilities of autonomous experimentation of the capacity for common self-management?

We can propose another hypothesis. Capitalist rationality is now trying to reconstruct, through financial mechanisms, the capacity to measure its own development. The concept of measure—unhinged, as we have seen, when linked to the labor theory of value—is thus recomposed under the illusion that financial measures might correspond to processes of real valorization. This is not the case. However, capitalist illusion is strong, and the efficiency of its command stronger still. The ways in which the multitude can take hold of financialization processes, or better yet, destroy their capacity for mystification remain to be thought out.

Let us set aside this digression for now, and return to the problem at hand. How does the concept of the common play out in the caesura between modernity and postmodernity, and between modern and imperial sovereignty? First of all, we must insist on the fact that *there is no continuity between the management of the* welfare state *and forms of antagonistic and/or multitudinous construction of the common.*

On this point, our hypothesis hinges on the reconstruction of a different measure, evoked in the second and third workshops. This measure is a construction, from the base, that appears once the traditional, objective, and temporal conditions of measure (linked to the classical labor theory of value) have disappeared.

In the following lectures, we will attempt to confront this problem. First, we will inquire as to whether the theme of measure (coinciding in capitalism with the theme of rationality) can be taken up again and further explored, or whether we should radically criticize it until its complete disappearance.

In the course of reconstructing the common, we might perhaps be brought back to the Spinozan theory of the "common name," to the material construction and the practice of the concept, as well as to the dimensions that organize and develop its social existence.

In that case, and to remain on philosophical terrain, the theme of the "common name" must be connected to that of singularization. Consequently, it shall have to be confronted with the linguistic processes qualifying the different moments of the cooperative constitution of the real.

Workshop 5

Postmodern Critique as Marginal Resistance

In the previous lectures, we have seen how insisting on the ontological and political caesura allows us to shine light upon the new, positive or negative characteristics of the emergence of the postmodern. We must now grasp the ambiguity of critical and philosophical reactions to modern ontology. The result of these reactions was primarily to dissolve the conceptual framings of modernity, a negating and negative function. Although the development of the critical process in postmodernity has been lengthy and important, it has remained *essentially negative and destructive.* Such negativity was central, of course, in order to create distance, and break with the past. But inasmuch as our inquiry concerns what *political* thought has become in the age of Empire, we must take into account the initial—and absolutely singular—characteristics of critical and philosophical postmodernity understood as the dissolution of modern political ontology, as well as all the positive alternatives it enables. We shall therefore try to understand, starting from this negative reaction *against* the modern, *how concepts and experiences of a new kind have also been proposed in an affirmative manner.*

In the course of this reconstitution, we shall have to move back and forth between philosophy and politics. This is clearly justified once it is understood that the metaphysics of modernity has always been an intertwining of philosophy and politics, and that its final result—the conception of the "autonomy of the political"—betrayed both modernity and postmodernity. We have already started demystifying the loosely defined notion of the "autonomy of the political" in previous workshops: for us, politics is never an absolute synthesis; rather, it is inevitably divided into power relations and resistance strategies. The "autonomy of the political" is thus an illusion upheld by power itself.

Again, we situate ourselves first of all by acknowledging the caesura between the modern and the postmodern. We will here favor the ambiguous aspects of that rupture, and concern ourselves with the weakness of the lines of flight it has incurred.

From this point of view, there are no better examples than those found in the philosophical positions of Lyotard, Baudrillard and Virilio. For these authors, the horizon is qualified by capitalism's total investment of life: by a biopower colonizing and occupying the entire biopolitical fabric of history and society, in other words, by a series of absolutely impassable effects and technological drifts (*dérives*). They believe there is nothing to be done. In their view (that some might, in part justifiably, consider paranoid), we circulate within an absolutely fetishized and commodified world. The moralizing stance of the Frankfurt school here becomes a relatively vulgar theory. It is translated in terms of a violent phenomenological transcription of fact, and, powerless to escape this descriptive dimension, almost seems to find its own weaknesses amusing. We thus find ourselves before an extremely objective and economist Marxism, subject to the "neocapitalist" ideology of modernity—as it sometimes appears in Debord's situationism—that it presupposes.

It is not necessary to further insist on this first postmodern perception of mature capitalism. *What is important is its acknowledgment of the totality of the totalitarian effects of biopower. What is unacceptable, and obsolete, is the critical weakness of its usage of "real subsumption of society under capital."* Not only does real subsumption of society under capital signify domination, it also signifies, and we have already insisted on this point, the global emergence of contradictions, antagonisms, and their discrepancy.

Such critical "weakness" becomes the fundamental characteristic (amoral, superficial, apologetic, individualistic) of what has been called the *postmodern apperception of the real*. Use value no longer exists; there is no possibility inherent in (and ensuing from) the world of commodities; our knowledge and souls are transformed into commodities. To escape this condition, we are left with conscious or unconscious witticisms, a few esthetic experiences, or some communitarian experiences outside of time. Escape becomes individualized, solitary, hidden. Beware of the dangers of the collective... *Bene vixit qui bene latuit*: he has lived well who has lived well hid—the seventeenth century libertine slogan returns as the symbol of today's philosophical thought and political experience. As it appropriates the materialist perception of reality, postmodern phenomenology forgets the joy of imagination and the power of revolt: thus is "weak thought" born.

Yet there is a great difference between these early positions of critical postmodernism *à la* Lyotard—with great documentary value, and witness to a kind of nostalgia of being, both resigned and enormously violent—and the emergence of what has been called "weak thought" in the seventies and eighties, in Europe and in the United States!

From Richard Rorty to Gianni Vattimo, the political version of weak thought appears rather than its phenomenological version. The question is not so much to show the depth of the crisis, phenomenologically, but to morally expose the scope of the defeat. *Weak thought, whether North American or European, is repenting, full of rancor, and blames itself for May 1968.* Its superficiality is flight, not even reactionary at that, reduced to the individualistic and private rediscovery of the mortal nature of man. But there is no tragedy in this, just a kind of monstrously stupid complacency. It is accompanied both by the pleasure of rediscovering oneself as servant and agent of biopower, and by the resentment of having lived rebellious moments, yet being incapable of absolutely wiping them from memory. Behind each sigh, each miniscule mumble, lays that little infamy of remorse and the rediscovery of transcendence (unavowed... and yet: how else can we understand the flight of the weak?). It is not the negative moment of a real dialectic. Neither is it the negative dialectic of the Frankfurt school—powerless and yet so strong. "Weak thought" is nothing else than the *repenting and opportunistic political expression of the postmodern caesura.* We must here emphasize its political, sentimental and moralistic traits rather than its ontological value.

It is also useful to recall the extent of the real (psychological and political) consequences of the philosophical crisis of such thought. From this perspective, this crisis follows from the more general crisis of Western Marxism, understood as the ideologies and practices of European communist parties. Weak thought is in fact the attempt to adapt philosophy to the modalities of socialist politics, to destroy any reminiscence of class struggle, and to make the metaphysical and epistemological structure of philosophy correspond to the incapacity to understand the forces quickening the real. We all know that the crisis of reformist socialism in the West and the crisis of "real socialism" in the East go hand in hand. Perhaps the only merit of weak thought is to have indicated a possible bridge between the tragic disillusions of Western reformism and the neoliberal fever arising from the crisis of Oriental Marxism. In both cases, however, the result is revolting.

In our analysis of postmodern thought, and its capacity/incapacity to recognize in a positive way the epochal passage we have lived through, we must also mention (and criticize) the singular perception shared by theoreticians of law and politics. Here, we refer in particular to three authors who have greatly influenced the juridico-political terrain, and have been considered figures of reference for a democratic thought that might recompose the image of postmodern reality: Luhmann, Habermas, and Rawls.

Here, notions of "public space" and of "public opinion" play a mystifying role. In the case of our three authors, we are faced with the extremely coherent acknowledgment of a negative *caesura*, an interruption, an interval, an empty space to fill: *that of political representation and of a new form of sovereignty*. It is not worth reviewing the specific development of the criticism of mature capitalism and its transcendental reconstruction, its rediscovery of the individual and its proposal for a sovereign generality. For our three authors, on the contrary, the issue is to consolidate—that is, to render irreducible—the modern theory of the state.

Luhmann formulates this passage as systemic; Rawls defines it contractually; Habermas characterizes it through a strange half-Kantian, half "young-Hegelian" transcendentality. In all cases, the problem seems to be that of ascribing a real consistency to the illusory image of public opinion, providing public space with a form of ethics, and consequently, consolidating the "democratic" conception of society, of the state, and of political representation. It is an attempt to erase the doubts that the postmodern apperception of the malleability of the values and ductility of sovereign relations might induce in relation to the efficiency of the liberal constitution in its classical, Western version.

All three authors, while they maintain the fullest, most irreversible acknowledgment of the postmodern caesura, hide the depth, pain, and radical nature of that passage under too many hot compresses...

Many have tried to read, in their critical consciousness, a tragic component of the epochal passage. In reality, it is the opportunistic justification of their unjustified support of a strongly criticized liberal, or neoliberal, ideology. We are free to choose our own historical and philosophical evaluation of such compromises!

Let us now shift our criticism from the ideological terrain—on which we have, up till now, been focused—to reality. What we need to grasp is *the effectiveness and maturity of postmodern categories.* First of all, the relation between use value and exchange value must be demystified. This is an old Marxist polemic, yet it is central to defining the postmodern. It is also at the heart of the rupture with a conception of politics and sovereignty issuing from the secular tradition as well as from the critique of the development of modernity. A new element, however, has been added to the discussion: the full acknowledgment that there can be no value outside of the world's commodification. The intensity of the immanentist approach to present history blocks all recourse to naturalist or essentialist conceptions of value. *No outside remains,* as we have often repeated. There is no nature or value to rely on. Yet we can act, and therefore destroy relativism: we can produce subjectivity. With postmodern philosophers, the world becomes contemporary once again: we must now construct its subjects.

In this regard, let us introduce an additional consideration. Alongside the attention given to real subsumption of society under capital, we find, in those philosophers who have defined the status of the postmodern in Europe and in the United States, *a reduction of use value to exchange value* represented in the dynamics and forms of "commodity fetishism." Such commodity fetishism (a Marxist theory that remained unchanged from the early writings to the *Capital*, that is to say, despite the refining of materialist critique) is considered fundamental and inescapable. However, for Marx, the "end of use value" and fetishism do not constitute the same moment, the same logical identity. Fetishism represents the point of view of capitalism according to which it is impossible to harness value outside of domination. Yet this point of view cannot remain as is once subjected to criticism. If we pay attention to capitalist development and to the evolution of social struggles (and moreover if we consider the biopolitical fabric that lies at the base of the contradictions and crises of biopowers), we must necessarily recognize that use value is modified beyond, and more deeply than, so-called "commodity fetishism."

In the anthropological historicity and substantial temporality characterizing the transformation of ways of life, use value is always recovered as a basic element. Although it is continually modified, it always remains fundamental to the revolutionary project (of radical transformation of the world). *The end of use value and commodity fetishism do not constitute an oxymoron.* Or, more precisely, the paradox that links them is greater than their conceptual homology, and use value continually reappears articulated with the desire for emancipation, the affirmation of subjectivities, and productive *potency (puissance)*. What remains of Marxism is the experience of use value understood in its relation to resistance and struggle.

The fetishistic transformations of capital are opposed to the *biopolitical metamorphoses* (technical, political, ontological) of the labor force. If you are looking for use value, you will not find it in naturalness but rather in history, in struggles, in the continual transformation of ways of life. *Use value is always reconstructed; it is always to the "nth" power.*

We have introduced this discussion on the difference between the critique of use value and its transformations (from the philosophical point of view) and the predominance of fetishism because of the questionings and ambiguities many authors have entertained on this point. Certain French poststructuralists—particularly Baudrillard and Virilio—consider the transformation of use value in an absolutely deterministic way. It thus becomes an irresolvable problem and an object undetectable in the transformation of modes of production, modes of life, and capitalist structure.

Giorgio Agamben and Jacques Derrida, in order to escape such reduction, try to uncover, at extreme margins, something giving itself as a residue of life—beyond exchange value's suffocation of use value. It is then a question of margins, of exodus, of flight, of liminal revolts...

Certain Italian Marxists such as Paolo Virno search for a concept of nature through which to reformulate the idea of use value, and revert to a kind of Chomskyan essentialism to escape the menace of relativism. From a certain point of view, we might say the same of Habermas' transcendental ambiguities...

But we shall return to this soon.

For us, on the contrary, the history we belong to offers no palingenetic possibility of salvation; nature is completely modified and artificialized by industrial technology and techniques of the production of subjectivity. Knowing this puts us "in situation," as the existentialists would have said. In that way, we can confront historical development and give concrete form to the paradoxes we encounter.

Let us allow ourselves another interruption. When we speak of the postmodern, and of that strange paradox that consists in recognizing ourselves within its compact structure without reducing use value to fetishism—or the total absorption of reality by domination—we introduce a creative element to our vision and our concrete assessment of the real. We have already spoken of this in regards to the excess of productive labor in today's mode of production, and to the irreducible character of living work in relation to the capitalist structure of domination. *In the words of Marx: "Use value is living labor."*

In the past, in modernity, we have faced analogous alternatives. These were, of course, inscribed in a different historical, political, and social context. Our aim is not to construct a general model of sorts, disregarding essential variations. However, it seems important to note that at different moments, traditions of thought—modern and postmodern—have confronted similar problems. Let us then simply examine this reference metaphorically, and read therein the troubling suggestion of an identical query.

Spinoza identified, in the density of being, the potential (*puissance*), the *dynamis* that renews being itself. This is the metaphor we mean to reclaim. *Dynamis* is living labor. *However, since living labor is use value, it is also the renewal of the potential* (puissance) *of use value.* What we are adding here ceases to be metaphorical; it becomes a philology (or, more precisely, *a genealogy*) of postmodern thought.

Unfortunately, postmodern thought has been conditioned by a perception of the present—and its corresponding definition of subjectivity—caught within a Heideggerian dimension of being. For Heidegger, *dynamis* and potential (*puissance*) are not synonymous with freedom. He does not consider them to be radically ontological constructive forces; they are inconclusive tendencies of human action, and literally tend towards nothingness. The inconsolable perception of being that is the postmodern viewpoint, although stemming from Marxist thought, arrives at a Heideggerian metaphysical conclusion: potential (*puissance*) cannot produce the new, it is completely blocked by nonbeing, and use-value is essentially reduced within exchange value. The postmodern, fetishized world cannot be breached.

It is here that Spinoza counters Heidegger, on this great theater of being and presence. The Spinozan potential (*puissance*) is opposed to the Heideggerian *Dasein*, in the same way as *amor* is opposed to *Angst*, *mens* to *Umsicht*, *cupiditas* to *Entschlossenheit*, *conatus* to *Anwesenheit*, *appetitus* to *Besorgen*...

We have already emphasized the fact that the Frankfurt School represents the direct and immediate precedent for all postmodern conceptions of the world. The Frankfurt School was, in fact, the most powerful of the Marxists revisionist schools. It irremediably disjoined the universal fetishism of commodities from the possibility of revolution, the latter being reduced to an eschatological perspective. Between fetishism and eschatology, the choice was impossible and desperate. We shall not insist on the Benjaminian origins of such despair. We very well understand why proclaiming the impossibility of revolution (based on the fetishism/eschatology alternative), that is, the impossibility of recuperating use value as revolutionary power, made Benjamin's positions fashionable. Of course, we are not questioning the value and coherence of Benjamin's thought, only its subsequent use. Let us remember what Bertolt Brecht said, in a poem that was both fraternal and critical, about his friend and comrade's decision to commit suicide.

Hannah Arendt has examined these issues in a caricaturing and sometimes provocative manner. Yet she has sometimes been hindered, however, because she fell *victim to a kind of liberal discourse* that presented itself as antitotalitarian, underlying the doctrine of Communist "*containment*" typical of Cold War political expression. Hannah Arendt's political discourse falls squarely within American strategies of obstructing and fighting realized socialism. Yet her philosophy is clearly not reducible to this. Her conception of democracy as the power of workers' councils, her theorization of the Shoah as a modern capitalist industrial product and a terrain for the expression of the "banality of evil," finally, her reading of American constitutionalism as the product of exodus and revolt, and as the profound experience of an "invention of politics," are essential elements of constructive and positive postmodern thought. However, what is unacceptable—and is always given as *auctoritas*— is the insistence on the linear production of democracy on the constitutional, political, liberal terrain as well as the edulcorated description of the revolutionary subjectivity at its base...

For Arendt, the last remaining "hopes" (and certainties) of democratic Occidentalism belonged to the same cosmology as fetishism, eschatology, the Frankfurt School, and Walter Benjamin. It is therefore easy to grasp the importance of that equivocal parenthesis in the post-modern perception of the crisis, and its destructive impact.

A few thinkers have refused to sail the subdued waters of the neoliberal usage of the postmodern. I am referring here to Derrida and Agamben. Both thinkers place themselves absolutely on the line when it comes to the radical caesura implied by postmodernity; both construct the idea of a possible resistance *against* the radical and totalitarian consistency of the capitalist subsumption of society. Theirs is an interesting moment in the history we are attempting to reconstruct, especially as our inquiry concerns the interval, the intermittent space, between the surrender to fate and the refusal (the decision, the ethical insurgency) to affirm freedom. Unfortunately, this difference remains marginal: it is only at the edge of a world entirely colonized by biopower that something like resistance can emerge. However, insisting on resistance, on the formidable invention of an irreducible singularity, acknowledges an essential creativity: that resistance produces, constructs, invents... Of course, neither Derrida nor Agamben posit this as such. Yet, their interests lie clearly in this margin, this edge, this fault line. Missing in Derrida is a positive and continuous phenom-enology that would transform the margin into creation. Missing in Agamben is a value that might distinguish between the anarchic lure of the void and the loving construction of the social (by loving, we mean *amor* as ontological power). However, both identify a space where resistance might actually take place.

In this workshop, we have perhaps too strongly emphasized certain theoretical and philosophical characteristics of the genesis and crisis of postmodernity (in fact, they are one and the same). In the following lecture, we shall try to define difference as a concrete historical subject. But what we have just seen was useful. It helped us clarify certain arguments, and mostly, allowed us to affirm their usefulness in regards to some of their instrumentations. Once again, how cruel is it to see Walter Benjamin or Hannah Arendt's theories used to construct a powerless postmodernity subject to neoliberal ideology. Yet this has been so often the case... In universities, in newspaper articles, Benjamin and Arendt provide the means for the construction of a disenchanted apology of the present. Critical function is reduced to the impossible game between utopian affirmation and eschatological metaphysics, between hopes of joy and the mystified, painful, and irresolute consciousness of ontological limits.

We disagree. All of this is false. The world is not how they describe it. And keeping our distance from any form of extremism, the simple and concrete possibility of transforming the world is still here.

Workshop 6

Difference and Resistance:
From the Postmodern Caesura to the Ontological Constitution of What is to Come (*a-venir*)

The previous workshop provided a methodological and historical analysis of several "events" of modernity and of its crisis. We must now reintroduce certain epistemic functions in order to explain our own becoming, that is, to take us from the postmodern caesura to the ontological construction of what is to come, or the possibility of reconstructing a postmodern antagonism. We shall therefore try to radically define—as we did in the first lectures of this series—certain concepts so as to describe our biopolitical context and to grasp the difficult question of *political decision*. The concepts of *difference*, separatism and/or separation, *resistance*, and *exodus* find their place here, as do, on another level, *hybridization*, *métissage*, "*creolization*," *metamorphosis*, etc. Our goal, of course, is not to provide rigid definitions. Rather, we shall work through successive problematizations, and show the breadth and depth of a novel mode of questioning rather than reconstruct a univocal key.

Until now, we have insisted on the ideological and political contradiction at the intersection of what we might call, on the one hand, the perception of the crisis of modernity and postmodern consciousness, and on the other, all the moral or theoretical lines of flight that tried to negate its obviousness, or the opportunistic or tragic detours it gave rise to. The entire generation of May 68 experienced this so intensely as to almost forget its tragic character.

Beyond such historical leveling off, we must now work towards *seeing the postmodern as a new world of resistance.* There is in fact a radical, and unbridgeable caesura between modernity and post-modernity. For our generation, there is no doubt about it. Doubts arise later, when it comes to defining what is to come. It is acknowledged that the postmodern conditions our life, that it is an historically determined and ontologically stabilized phase. Yet this condition is the product of the real subsumption of society under capital, whereas our task today is to acknowledge the specificity of the antagonistic characteristics of the postmodern.

This is, in reality, a difficult and complex issue. What does "antagonism" mean in a society that is dominated by commodity fetishism and colonized by capitalism, that is, in a society charac-terized by real subsumption? What do we mean by "resistance" in the age of Empire? These are not simply theoretical problems. They are also the specific determinations of the historical process, and articulations of what collective wishes emerge there. Such determi-nations are collective, and such wishes, revolutionary decisions. In any case, this is what we believe. We have never been told (nor will we be told before a revolutionary process is set in motion) *what building democracy, freedom, equality and wealth means* in a world that capitalism thinks it can asphyxiate by annihilating all possibility of resistance.

When speaking of real subsumption, we often provided the archeology of the concept, that is, we considered the process leading from modernity to postmodernity historically. We thus insisted on its genealogical analysis, so as to account for the ontology of the contemporary. We were well rewarded by genealogical intelligence. For economists, and for philosophers as well, the shock of the transition has been central. However, instead of recognizing that the ontology of today's world is irreversible, and therefore targeting its meaning and tendencies, they have often preferred to analyze the dynamics of its transformation. Thus, the specific, singular characteristics of the new phase seemed fleeting and confused.

Michel Foucault's work, starting from the early 80s, was in this regard absolutely different and innovative. His research provided a precious means of escape from the state of paralysis instigated by the rediscovery of ontology. *But enough with the genealogy of the postmodern. Let us insist at present on the ontology of today's world,* that is, on a dimension of the contemporary that no hermeneutics can reduce.

In order to reconstitute the importance of the postmodern caesura, two philosophical trajectories are of great importance: that of Gilles Deleuze and of Michel Foucault. Around 1968, Deleuze, who had already written that masterpiece, still inscribed within French structuralism, called *Difference and Repetition*, also reinvents philosophical critique by concentrating its meaning through a theoretical line prefigured by his work on expression and potential (*puissance*) in Spinoza. The desire to break with tradition and the reinvention of subjectivity—Deleuze reads them as attempts to exalt difference against repetition and affirm singularity against universal abstraction—will be later given in *Anti-Oedipus*, written with Felix Guattari, as a positive reversal of Freudian libido. This is precisely the point where their conception of ontological difference is reconstructed. We shall return to this shortly, as we attempt to articulate difference, resistance, and creativity.

For now, let us debate *the possibility of a positive alternative within the postmodern.*

Deleuze maintained that a subjective activity passes through the real, regardless of the level of colonization of the real by capital. On this point, he stood opposed to the Frankfurt School and the opaque revisionism of the later Marxists. Consequently, there had to be a virtuality, perhaps even a real possibility, of transforming this new subjectivity into resistance. What had to be refused was the shift that might allow those figures affirming their own radical difference—weak or strong, but always antagonistic—to be confused with the figures of a being that had been rendered powerless. Neither could subjectivity be allowed to lose itself in the postmodern context, and be dissolved in the flat circulation of commodities and significations. The resisting subject emerged as an inventor of meaning, as the synthesis of intelligence and cooperation.

The fact is that the apparatuses (*dispositifs*) of singular *cupiditas* (those active projections of subjectivity on the biopolitical horizon) were not only represented from a critical standpoint: desire became considered as something else than just the movement of the principle of existence. Existence was once again totally caught up in the intensity of phenomenological experience and could therefore be epistemologically harnessed as creating ontological difference. However, *cupiditas* was also understood both as absolutely singular and different, and absolutely differential in itself, that is, irreducible to primary terms. This was an essential point that Deleuze emphasized in *Difference and Repetition,* and that he went on to develop in the two volumes of *Capitalism and Schizophrenia* written with Félix Guattari.

Foucault intervenes precisely on this point. He immediately grasps what is at stake in Deleuze and Guattari, and says so: *Anti-Oedipus* is a flash that coincides with the decision of a radical modification for thought in the twenty-first century. He sees, in the strange and powerful game that fascinates him in Deleuze, the need to move from the surface to the ontological ground (*fond*). Foucault reinserts *the ontology of production into the biopolitical fabric*. Foucaldian archeology and genealogy thus become active players in a theory of the production of being. It is an incredible intuition.

Let us look at how this theoretical decision is instigated. Foucault had long kept company with structuralism. He had been a kind of Parisian theoretician of the Frankfurt School. Suddenly, at the end of the 60s, for reasons we cannot analyze here, he feels the need to *subjectivize the lines of flight* that the "resistant margins" (as Derrida would say) had opened within the postmodern. This necessity—the difference represented by the experience of transgression—must be transformed into genuine activity: subjectivity must define itself as its own actor. It is around this question that we can distinguish two phases in Foucault's work. Regardless of the polemics that try to flatten the permanent renewal of Foucault's thought into a gray, homogenous continuity, it is clear that the "production of subjectivity" is a reinvention of freedom within postmodern conditions of subjection and domination. Admittedly, such freedom is different. It is nonformal, yet it can act within the totality of biopolitical space, of which it is both the condition of possibility and the effect.

Although it might seem paradoxical, Foucault arrives at the following idea: when power spreads to all social relations (regardless of their nature), and consequently, when we switch from the old dichotomous structure of class relations to a finer, less visible, and infinitely more efficient analytics of powers, antagonism also spreads to the social world in its entirety and reaches each stitch in the fabric it is made of... This passage is essential. It does not consist in seeing potency (*puissance*) everywhere, but in identifying the antagonism in that space spreading between potency and power, in the finest links of the social fabric, and in all the articulations of political power. *Foucault brings the desire and libido of* A Thousand Plateaus *into social antagonism and political struggle.*

We must now return to the relation between difference, resistance, and creativity, and to its epistemological determination. We wish to formulate the idea that this relation lies at the heart of the political discourse of postmodern philosophy. Of course, it could be objected that all metaphysics immediately imply a political dimension, even in the modern period, and this is true. The metaphysics of modernity is a theory of power (it is also a *figure* of power, an *image*, the *specter* of biopowers). Today, however, the mediations through which power appears, be they metaphysical or imaginative, are disappearing. What is emerging is the ontology of power. *When we confront the centrality of the political in postmodernity, we are directly confronting an ontological problem.* But what ontology, then, are we speaking of?

The ontological problem is directly rooted in the relation between difference and creativity. Our hypothesis is as follows: resistance is what allows for the existence of a relation between both terms. But if difference and creativity are ontological, then resistance will be so as well. However, all this does not explain the nature of the relations that exist between the three. It is necessary to grasp the ontological nature of the passage from difference to creativity at the heart of resistance. We must therefore denaturalize difference. We must disintegrate any element that might recreate a corporate or identity-based movement within the passage from difference to creativity, and understand the latter as a moment that is diffusive and versatile, changing and powerful, constant and forever reinvented. Resistance is what allows difference and creativity to be intertwined. That is what the *clinamen* consists in; it is introduced once we acknowledge difference. From the temporal point of view, it can be defined as the *kairòs* of the activity of resistance. By *kairòs*, we mean the powerful irruption of time in the relation between difference and creativity. The *kairòs* is the instant of creation, the moment potential (*puissance*) spreads on the edge of being, that is, the capacity to invent within the framework of the postmodern. We insist: *everything occurs on the edge of being*—not on the limit, in the margins of a given ontological totality, but in each moment that makes up the passage from difference to creativity. On the edge of being: *because the edge is everywhere*.

But why go towards the unknown in this way? Because the unknown is the phenomenological dimension of the postmodern, because it is our condition, the condition of those searching for a way to reconstruct a meaningful horizon of life in a world of commodities with no "outside." Ethical risk is the counterpart to the epistemic unknown, and the phenomenology of the postmodern, as we have often described it, takes hold of the edge of being. On the edge of being, radical immanence precludes any possibility of teleology and imposes the radical responsibility for what is to come, in order to make a sensible reconstruction of life possible. Consequently, radical immanence affirms itself through the refusal of the homologizing violence of power, and by acknowledging that only singularities can bring forth the common. Once again: biopolitical potential (*puissance*) against biopowers.

On this issue, we might note that certain feminist discourses of the second half of the twentieth century that insisted on separatism as a weapon against patriarchy were based on the same *difference* we are speaking of here, and greatly elaborated on the creative apparatuses (*dispositifs*) this difference permitted. We shall return to this question soon.

When we speak of difference, we are therefore speaking of resistance. Difference cannot be recognized within the homologation that biopower imposes on society. When we speak of difference, we mean the way resistance emerges against the compact mass of biopower in order to affirm the common consistency of the biopoliticial fabric. It is only through the continuous renewal of this fabric, through creativity, life styles, and the destruction of all forms of essence or identity that difference can be affirmed, and *the common constructed*. The common is nothing but all these movements conjoined.

Let us now go back to the years following 1968, when these problems were posed in a decisive manner.

It was often in a very repressive context that difference—feminist of course, but let us also keep in mind the plethora of its productive usages—started to function fully as *separation*. Difference corresponded to the preliminary moment of constitution of a subjectivity separating itself in order to exist. It is true that difference has been considered—quite realistically—an extremely difficult political practice, since separation alone allows for action. From the workers' point of view, for example, this led to a kind of heroism in the defense of politics—including terrorism of the most desperate sort; in reality, separation severed contact with the real social base of struggles. For that matter, feminism often led to the absolute disaster of private (family or emotional) lives shunted and set aside. Separation became the forgetting of the self since the relation to the other was forgotten. It would be useful to conduct a radical political critique of solitude, of withdrawal into the self, or, more political yet—albeit not so different—of the blind and sometimes despairing narcissism of the avant-garde.

However, once this moment of crisis had passed—a crisis that most often led to suicide and self-destruction rather than to a real transformation of living conditions—difference started constructing itself differently, creatively. *In certain cases, there is no doubt that separation was historically necessary*: precisely because it was historically determined, and an occasion not to be missed. *Yet it was not sufficient.* A comparison with the history of anarchism might be made, in that anarchism represented a necessary yet insufficient condition when it came to building a true communist perspective in the context of the genesis of the modern working class.

In the end, separation is a position/decision that remained inscribed within the history of "*raison d'Etat*," within the continuity of emancipatory processes internal to power itself. Separation participated in power, even (and mostly) when it wished to break the symmetry between resistance and power. To repeat, I firmly believe that separation, although it constitutes a necessary moment in the trajectory of subjectivities, remains internal to power. *The constitutive and creative process only really begins when separation becomes productive difference, and not just subtraction. It begins when there is no longer the need to take power, because the development of the potential* (puissance*) of difference is affirmed.*

This difference, beyond the contradictory characteristics of separation, is one that can immediately influence the affective nature and passionate dimensions of collective living. From this point of view, separatism represented the first important moment in thinking and practicing difference. From the point of view of the production of subjectivities, separatism was one of the main elements that brought to light the historical caesura between modernity and postmodernity. It implied innovative ways of life and creative attempts at the self-production of singular or collective subjectivities, radically breaking with the characterizations of modernity. Consequently, separation corresponded to a partial reinvention of politics that anticipated the creativity of biopolitics.

When, for example, women and workers decide to separate—from the patriarchal organization of society on the one hand, and from the stronghold of capital on the other—and organize their own exodus, something happens that is not simply a theoretical affirmation. Something becomes ontological.

It would be unjust to refer simply to the historical effects of these struggles, and to the paradoxical way in which power relations have reorganized around them. In the 70s, the extension of womens' rights and the affirmation of workers' rights was an enormous victory, even though both cases proved the failure of separatism. Clearly, thirty-five years later, what we remember of these great processes of subjectivation is how they inaugurated and practiced the affirmation of difference beyond separation. It is on such bases, and in an ontological manner, that we must once again take up difference (issued from separation), resistance, and creativity.

Let us first insist on the importance of this alternative born out of the 70s, and examine it more closely.

At the time, subjects of sexual and economic reproduction built a common movement that finally culminated in the practice of separatism, understood as a necessary means to affirm their interest in living and (self-) reproducing. Yet, for affirmation to become productive, paradoxically, it was necessary to negate the identity that was possessed before. Difference was this negation. It was an extremely rich and necessary negation, even though it could not escape its own failure. Just as life searches for new paths when it is faced with an obstacle, the subjects we are speaking of here reacted by trying out new practical trajectories. They tried the way of exodus. But this exodus also had to become productive.

This brings us to a first definition of *exodus as creative separation*. However, in the opposition between identity/separation and difference/creativity that lies at the heart of resistance—that is, in the sequence of exodus—we see the emergence of one of the most problematic and important elements of processes of postmodern liberation. *This element is decision.*

Let us look at the feminist question, the affirmation of sexual difference, resistance to patriarchy and to its values, and the negative moment of separation... It is when separatism becomes difference that the capacity for exodus arises. By this we mean the capacity to reconstruct an entire world from passionate, personal, social, civil, historical, and political differences that were invented in separation. Our world is too heavy to blast at once. It is too complex for us to dream of a Winter Palace to conquer. So *we must leave, and construct new forms of life*, new articulations and novel trajectories within the social field. Feminism gave an important interpretation of this strategy. But, once again, we ask, when did the moment of decision occur?

Before getting to the heart of the problem, please allow us one last comment on feminism, concerning the naturalist dimension of difference on which it is sometimes, unfortunately, based. The emphasis on naturalist characteristics in certain feminist currents is purely reactionary. Militant feminism, on the contrary, has transformed natural difference into cultural and historical difference, thus translating it into a new kind of creative ontology. New currents in radical feminism from the 1990s—from Judith Butler to Donna Haraway—have a tendency to eliminate "naturalist" difference, and to follow the path of metamorphoses and gender hybridization. The exodus process is clear. And again, we ask: where do we encounter decision?

The same problem comes up when we consider *the resistance of the labor force and the workers' revolt* of the 70s. In that case as well, we are confronted with an identity that affirms itself at the start: a working class, a strong, mature, white male labor force, a brutish pagan species whose separation has become the most effective negotiating power, and beyond that, something that might topple the balance of capitalist reproduction. Of course, that experience went hand in hand with a measure of corporatism. Again, we cannot underestimate the elements of naturalization that separation entailed. A strange naturalism indeed... In fact, it was a kind of economism that had borrowed its fixity and teleology from true naturalism... What it tried to do was to define, through separation, a position of autonomy and absolute independence, of what, in the relation of capital to reformist dialectics, was traditionally given as a continuous flow tied to development.

This separation was a success. It was a kind of Keynesianism, reversed and reformed according to the workers' point of view—at a time when struggles around salary had become *independent variables* of economic development. This demand for identity through separation also underwent moments of crisis, failure, and reformulation.

However, it defined new areas of struggle and novel forms of production: it was a kind of subterranean river that had understood the impossibility of the dream of separation, and knew that the only way to be present in the world of production was to develop from separation defined as a force enabling ever-changing transformations. In the midst of the conflicts that characterize the passage from modernity to postmodernity, Fordism to post-Fordism, separation gives way to a *General Intellect*: an immaterial, intellectual, linguistic, and cooperative work force that corresponds to a new phase of productive development based on the excess of work, or, in other words, on the creativity of living work. Thus living labor reconnects with the productive cycle. It had left through separation; it reenters with hegemony.

Just as the terms of the gender struggle have changed, so have all the parameters of the class struggle been modified and transformed.

Let us insist on the issue of the workers' separation one last time. On the one hand, there is the relation between the industrial, capitalist, and Fordist organizations of labor. On the other, there is the exodus of the labor force that occurs through a new class composition, new modes of life, and novel biopolitical practices. This issue gives us *a second definition of exodus*. As we have seen, the first definition insisted on the image of the path or trajectory; it appeared both as a refusal and as a new subjective deployment. The second, on the contrary, insists on the end point of the trajectory, on the consolidation of a new structure of existence, *a new ontological figure*.

We have already spoken of the passage from material to immaterial labor. It is marked not only by a change in the mode of production, by the transformation of the labor force and the discovery of its capacity to create value, but also by the new kind of exploitation running through immaterial work, by the modification of ways of life, by the change in the horizon of existence and its new qualification as a biopolitical condition.

When we speak of difference in this perspective, we do not mean difference simply as resistance. Here, *difference/resistance appears as the condition of possibility of the production of new subjectivities*, that is to say, as the condition of possibility of creation. At issue is not the illusion of identity, but, on the contrary, the acknowledgment—that exodus enables—of a new social terrain on which to organize, through revolt and resistance, the very existence of subjectivities. This is how we arrive at a new definition of exodus—because exodus, in this case, means to travel the entire space of the difference of material to immaterial labor, conquering anew the creative capacity that lies at the heart of living work. But how can this resistance to exploitation be transformed into an anticapitalist revolution? How can separation give way to *the radical alternative that revolutionary exodus represents?* We shall come back to these problems in the next lectures, for we shall have to tackle the problem of decision, and give it its rightful place.

In particular, we shall have to return in greater depth to the criticism leveled against the concept of multitude understood as a new category of political thought that corresponds to the novel subjective consistency we have detected. We are here referring to doubts formulated by Pierre Macherey concerning the multitude's capacity to build a decision and a unity of perspective, to those of Etienne Balibar, and to the refusal to consider the multitude as an antisystemic power in a world globalized by neoliberalism. We also have in mind Laclau or Rancière's objections as to the multitude's incapacity to provide a key to exodus that would be "political" and not simply material, and through which it could attain social hegemony.

Earlier, we mentioned hybridization in reference to a feminine subject caught between separation and difference. The term gave us the means to encounter, within difference itself, a point of view and a capacity for action that might together rearticulate *gender* and the production of subjectivity. In that perspective, metamorphosis and hybridization meant a new productive form.

Let us now consider the term from *the workers' point of view*. Hybridization is the crossing of the body and the intelligence, of the collective body and singular intelligences, of messages and linguistic cooperation, etc. The problem we are faced with appears at an ontological level, inasmuch as it concerns subjective metamorphosis. As is the case in feminism, the question posed by hybridization is in reality the problem of a new "*common*": a *new "nature"* —very strange indeed, since it is neither primordial nor original—that is the effect of a continuous production... In the case at hand, this production corresponds to the construction of a General Intellect and to the new nature of living work. We shall return to these themes in order to understand how the transformation of the labor force operates within emancipatory processes and allows living work to break the chains of its forced reduction under the power of capital.

All of this leads us to a *third definition of the word "exodus."* It must not only be understood as a path, a kind of ontological "deposit" or the slow accumulation of subjectivation processes. It is metamorphosis. More precisely, only because it is all these things can it become *metamorphosis*. Let us try to understand its mechanism.

Here, the notions of creolization and *métissage* we mentioned at the beginning of the workshop come into play. In order to confront these terms, we must move from an intensive dimension (productive separation and resistance) to an extensive, spatially determined dimension containing territorial flows, subjective mobility, and the transformations and metamorphoses operating within all the new forms of contiguity or contamination.

When we come upon such phenomena, we find ourselves thrown into the midst of the formidable multitudinous movements that characterize today's world. Entire worlds are concerned by migratory phenomena, entire populations are mobilized by the structural imbalances of global economy: *that is how multitudes are transformed*. Such transformations concern not only the Mediterranean basin and the Atlantic world—as was often the case historically—but the planet as a whole. Reality is molded by the growth of *métissage*. The strength of migrations—the passions that flow through them—is not only a trace of present transformations but also its essential and novel figure: a figure made of creative, intercultural, mingled crossings that alone can open the "great path of the world's *common*." Contrary to what old materialism taught us, territorial movements are just as decisive as structural transformations. But that is another discussion...

To conclude this lecture, let us summarize the problems we have addressed and that remain open. The first is, undoubtedly, the problem of "*decision*." Until now, our discourse on politics has been slightly ambiguous: we have always considered it under the angle of collective construction, as something constituting the very life of collectivity. Why do we insist on adding a voluntary, collectively effective and yet singularly constructed prosthesis such as decision to this anthropological constitution, this ontological process, this biopolitical character, and this necessary hybridization?

Decision seems to define the passage within the flow of the labor force (intensively, based on the transformations of the labor force; extensively, in migratory processes; and qualitatively, in processes of production) that provides a kind of subjective bridge between lived and enacted transformation. *The political dimension of decision is thus always double*: on the one hand, it presents itself as *a social determination*, on the other, as *a political act*. Of course, we shall have to return to all of this: the postmodern redefinition of the political probably hinges on this difficult point.

Moreover, the theme of decision implies other terms of even greater difficulty, those of "poverty" and "love."

When speaking of difference, we are speaking of creativity. But when we speak of creativity, we immediately refer to the singular and absolute relation that exists between wealth and *poverty*, between the wealth of difference and the poverty of power relations. This relation between wealth and poverty is completely positive: we shall soon see how it necessarily connects to the concept of love.

Workshop 7

From the Right to Resistance

to Constituent Power

In the previous lecture, we tried to understand how the right to resistance was grounded in the fabric of postmodern ontology, that is, in the web of difference and exodus. But speaking of "right" is not quite adequate, unless we redefine the reality and the meaning of the word "rights," and "law," in today's historical context of the passage into the postmodern.

Demanding a right entails affirming a subjective demand as a guarantor of legitimate behavior. To speak of legal rights is therefore, in a certain sense, to ground this demand within an objectively determined system of values. In what we have observed up to this point, it seems quite difficult to establish a relation between these two poles, since that demand must find its place between a subjective apparatus (*dispositif*) and an objective structure. In the traditional language of law, legitimacy is established precisely between claims and tutelage. The point we wish to criticize is the very possibility of affirming a universal form of legitimation. Based on this difficulty, we must attempt a new reasoning on law (and perhaps establish a new definition).

What interests us here above all is reforming the political lexicon, specifically as it concerns such notions as "subjective right," "citizenship," "the exercise of constituent power," or "democracy."

Of course, these terms being intricately connected to one another, it is difficult to define one without having to define the rest. We shall begin with them.

Let us start from the definition of what is understood as "subjective right," where we probably find what is closest to the "right to resistance." The right to resistance, as we have seen, has gone through many formulations. Almost all of these were based on a hierarchy attributing an unquestionable legitimacy to natural values, which in fact enabled the ties of obedience, at the base of the very notion of law in the Ancien Regime, to be broken. In the modern period, following the affirmation of republicanism on the part of Calvinist sects and contemporary to the Catholic response they received, the most important motivations for the right to resistance were provided by Catholic or Calvinist *monarchomac theories*. In those theories, the right to resistance was linked to categories of unilateral reference, fixed and closed upon themselves, as they were absolute values based in theology.

At the other extreme of possible definitions of the right to resistance, we find theories of anarchic inspiration, the other great source of the concept. These are characterized by the exclusion of all theological or transcendental referential contexts, yet they affirm the absolute character of disobedience and of the subversive anti-monarchic act. In this case, we are faced with the self-justification of resistance as such.

Once we have recognized this double lineage, we must return it to its right dimension. Today, in the context of the transition towards the postmodern, the right to resistance is neither absolute nor self-justified. It is rather a right built upon common demands and social cooperation. In that sense, it is built on the same bases as the affirmation of singularity that characterizes the common cooperative fabric, and the ontological tendency towards the common that singularities possess.

In modern public law, subjective rights appears under two forms: on the one hand, as the immediate and irreducible affirmation of certain fundamental rights pertaining to life, and consequently, to security and property; and on the other, as a subjective public right, entailing the legitimate demand for the expression of political freedom. By subjective public right, we mean the subjective political right, that is, the right to participation, representation, administration, and in general, to the control of functions of state. In the modern period, subjective rights are thus subsumed under public law, at the heart of state law, as the latter guarantees the tutelage of citizens and fosters the development of subjective rights through state organization. Clearly then, subjective law codifies the rights of the individual property owner, and consequently, it is an expression of the bourgeoisie and of its power to appropriate individual freedom and the market, and protect its prerogatives. This is what is expected of the state through the constitution, and what the state must guarantee and develop.

If we return to the identification we started out with, between the right to difference (the right to express one's own singularity) and the right to resistance, and if we remember that today, singularity is primarily expressed through cooperation, we arrive at a profoundly different definition of subjective rights. *At the heart of the multitude, subjective rights are not simply the defense of individual interests* (it is rather the opposite, since the interests of a singularity are difficult to recognize outside of its relation to another): *instead, they consist in the desire that cooperation, the collective power of the production of value and wealth be acknowledged.* If the multitude is a collection of singularities, and if the common is the ever-changing, ever-mobile, ever-renewed product of these singularities, then subjective rights henceforth imply the right to the shared informing of the processes that construct the common, and are the acknowledgment of the role of singularities within these processes.

The subjective public right must therefore be defined as what gives claim to *exercise the common*. It is given beyond all reference to a naturalist, identitary, or individualist base, that is, something that would exalt the private dimension of personal interest. On the contrary, it affirms a common interest that is the result of processes of cooperation, of the associative development of bodies, of the progress of struggles. The subjective right mediates between the "poverty" of the singular human condition upon entering the social context and "love" as associative power: it allows singularities to escape the world of pure needs.

But we do not live in an ideal epoch, and the different developments that singularities produce encounter obstacles and oppositions. *We encounter, in the construction of subjective rights, certain elements that characterize the right to resistance.* Affirming subjective rights is not an irenic operation. Yet the desire for peace must nonetheless *also* take into account the need to overcome the blocks and oppositions that try to halt its movement. Subjective rights must therefore immediately be recognized as determining antagonism. Acknowledging themselves as resistant, subjective rights affirm themselves precisely *because they are produced in antagonism*.

On this point, we dive once again into the midst of the Spinozan genealogy of law: *tantum iuris quantum potentiae*, Spinoza tells us. Between the tendency towards the common and emerging differences, it is the *conatus*, the *appetitus*, and the *cupiditas* that propose a law that might represent the production and establishment of ever-higher levels of social cooperation. In the Spinozan experience, the genesis of law is consequently everything but irenic. That Spinoza constructs the concept of multitude more as a conceptual reality than as a historically consistent phenomenon in no way alters this affirmation.

We must insist here on the necessity of concretizing subjective rights. This concretization—embodiment, territorialization—can be read differently according to several figures. *The first of these figures is diachronic.* In this case, we must establish what forms ontological specifications and strata of common existence take in the constitution of subjective law, and the present condition of this constitution.

Secondly, concretizing subjective rights implies their development in space, which means that we must define a concept of citizenship that corresponds to the present situation—according to Empire and its capacity to dissolve the borders and territorial conditions of public law.

Thirdly, concretizing subjective rights implies considering them according to a temporal perspective, or better yet, a genealogical one. This means understanding how subjective law, because it takes shape, becomes collective and is decided. How it becomes the collective body of the multitude and the holder of *constituent power*. We must then also understand how constituent power is formed, how it appears in the recent history of the liberation of singularities, how it emerges and is lodged at the heart of conditions that are more dissipated and centrifugal than homogenous and centripetal, how it sparks processes that transform the dispersal of singularities into the regrouping of the common.

Finally, we must understand how all of these lines crisscross and weave a complete redefinition of the very concept of democracy, giving it novel weight in the social and political mutations of today.

The first theme we shall investigate is the "diachronic disjunction" of subjective law, understood in its relation to the right to resistance. By diachronic disjunction we mean the difference that subjective law puts forward when it relates to ontological reality and to the latter's institutional specifications. These vary according to the contradictory process of institutional life: caught between subjective juridical demands and the state tutelage of these demands, they are configured by bases and articulations that are always different. The distinction between "*formal*" and "*material*" constitution, that is, the difference between the formal figure of the constitutional norm and all the forces and subjects materially determined by the constitution, is based on this diachronic gap, an opening that is always to be redetermined. This implies that the definition of subjective rights and the capacity to exert the right to resistance vary according to the relation between formal and material constitution: a subjective right can be abolished or another adopted. We are here describing a state of affairs and find ourselves on the field of a formal indetermination of institutional equilibriums. In fact, this relation is always open. There are times when the demands for formal rights is opposed to—or prevails over—the definition of material rights, and vice-versa: constitutional history represents this ontological variation, punctually determined—decided—by its historical conditions.

The theme of hegemony basically corresponds to these intertwined problems. Regardless of how we interpret the concept of "hegemony," everything is played out here. It is clear that when Gramsci speaks of hegemony, he transforms it into a kind of "dictatorship of the proletariat" (as Lenin does: "much more democratic than bourgeois democracy"). It is clear as well that Mouffe and Laclau, on the contrary, provide a purely sociological interpretation of hegemony, as if it could be defined as a *majority of public opinion* and as if its functioning could be organized *transcendentally* within civil society. But in both cases, what is at stake is always the relation between formal and material constitution.

Let us now look at the problem from the point of view of current political events (that is, from the point of view of Empire and the forms of exploitation characteristic of postmodern production). We can define this diachronic rhythm as the random dynamics of antagonism. "Open" and democratic constitutions are normally forced to listen to the expression of antagonism—in order to better absorb and control it. We are therefore on the historical ground that is characteristic of the postmodern period. This means that subjective demands (and even more so the right to resistance) are always contained within historical dynamics that transmute and metamorphose the terms of the debate according to the modifications registered by forms of cooperation.

If we move from the formal and/or material level of constitution to the analysis of the modes of production implicitly linked to it, we notice that the constitution and definition of subjective rights as well as the very proposal of the right to resistance are conditioned, in reality, by the modes of production. From a diachronic and historical point of view, we are in *a transitional period*, a period in which the paradigms and criteria of liberal-bourgeois constitutionalism are under discussion. The variations experimented in this context represent possible models for an efficient analysis of the dynamics of subjective law. It is not surprising that the struggles at the heart of biopower (between the powerful and those they subject, that is, within life as a social and productive complexity) appear as struggles between different formulations of subjective rights. What interests us foremost is understanding up to what point resistance might be modified within this temporal and historical rhythm, and consequently, today. But we shall return to this point soon.

The *theme of citizenship* allows us to verify the spatial development of subjective rights, understood as *the key problem of the contemporary period*. Citizenship is going through a profound crisis: its territorialization is becoming increasingly difficult as it is faced with migratory movements, continental and transcontinental exodus, intermixing and all the transformations of productive cooperation.

The crisis of the criteria of measure and/or regulation of such phenomena has been thoroughly studied. But in reality, it is around two fundamental elements that the notion of citizenship must be rethought: first, as it confronts the problems of emigration, globalization, and the erasure/exhaustion of borders—and more generally all spatial limits hindering the mobility of the work force; second, as it relates to the theme of immaterial production (that is, to capital and to the cognitive work force). We have seen an analogous phenomenon in the passage from the patrimonial state to the capitalist-industrial one. Yet this is even more visible today as the mode of production is based on the (relative) autonomy of immigrations and of immaterial work (intellectual, scientific, affective, etc.), both considered leading productive forces. The idea of *welfare* as it was implied in the development of territorial and/or liberal juridical thought is no longer operative. Within the modern (national) constitutional process, we can no longer account for a society that has seen the spread of the hegemony of the capitalist model of the wage relation as an organizational instrument of social production. Globalization and the movements that arise from it have bewildered citizenship.

However, a *"new" principle of citizenship* can still be affirmed. By new, we mean built upon the new reality of mobility and flexibility of labor in emigration and production. The critical genesis of the *welfare* state is completely linked to the affirmation of the autonomy of labor and migratory movements. The latest reactionary attempts consist in pitting these movements against each other: immigrants supposedly rob the labor of nationals, but on the other hand, workers are subject to rules of flexibility and mobility that no longer correspond to maintaining an independent national work force. On the contrary, these rules answer to the necessity, by capital/state, of establishing a hierarchy within the global movements of the labor force and, precisely, of harnessing, expropriating and exploiting this new mobility.

We can propose a new concept of citizenship only if it opposes—more exactly, if it resists—these imperial injunctions: by interiorizing, subsuming and structuring the social and biopolitical dimensions of the new productive actors (*citizenship then means: citizenship revenue*) as well as the mobile dimension of the productive subject (citizenship then means: the end of the attribution of rights through the right of blood or a right of soil applied to the work market). There is, finally, a third perspective according to which citizenship rights must necessarily be modified: that of the globalization of relations of communication in all sectors of global production.

In all of these cases, citizenship is severely questioned. Yet it is also invited to renew itself and to find another measure, *under the impetus of the new valorization processes* at work in intellectual, scientific, and affective labor on a global scale.

To summarize, once the territorial dimension of citizenship is shattered by globalization, it becomes a cosmopolitan project—even if we are just at the beginning of the transformation of citizenship. The second essential element at play is the acknowledgment of the common potential (*puissance*) of material labor, and of the expansive, intellectual, mobile, and flexible dynamics through which it is expressed. The territoriality of processes of capitalist sovereignty and valorization is compromised not only by the global movements of the labor force, but also, and mostly, by the intensity of globalization and by the new figure of the productivity of the work force. The crisis of citizenship follows that movement: *territorial* citizenship, the fundamental element constituting the modern state, is swept into an irremediable crisis.

We can be certain to grasp the depth of this crisis if we consider the relation of the attribution of citizenship to the exercise of subjective rights. Naturally, it is also through this gap between formal and material constitution, that is, the gap between the juridical conditions of command and the material conditions of subjectivity, that repressive forces strike. Thus, if citizenship also means the right to resistance, this right is, in reality, granted only to territorialized individuals, and not to migrants. More explicitly yet, only territorialized corporations (unions, associations, or groups based on ethnicity, etc.) can exert the public subjective right to resistance. *Everything else will be considered "terrorism."*

The concept of citizenship has crumbled due to its incapacity to understand and integrate the processes of globalization and productive intensification of immaterial work. A new citizenship is possible—and its parameters are clear—yet it remains considerably utopian in today's capitalist development. But we shall see...

In its traditional definition, it is not just the relation of citizenship to space that is perturbed. Its relation to time as well is implied: its constitution, its definition. When we refer back to constitutional texts, public subjective law gives the right to active participation in processes of government and administration. *Political representation is a fundamental subjective public right.* Here, however, representation is essentially understood within the limits of a "popular" function that reproduces the existing constitutional system. Do we ever wonder if such criteria really allow for the definition of public subjective law? How can the right to resistance—and the right to demand more or less radical transformations of the political and constitutional system—be taken into account? If we are correct in our interpretation of the diachronic dimension of subjective law, then the question is absolutely fundamental.

There is a conceptual reference in the dogma of public state law that might answer to this: *constituent power.* Constituent power is the capacity of the public structure of powers to renew itself; it is the capacity to propose and affirm new public dimensions within the distribution of these powers; it is a radical innovation of the formal constitution based on a radical reformulation of the material constitution.

This right, that might become a power, is recognized in principle. In reality, however, it is excluded from the constitutional dimension and the juridical procedures of state reform, from its constitution and its materialization. There are different figures that constituent power—meaning the reinforcement of public subjective rights—can take. For the most part, constitutional literature has established their characteristics. Yet beneath all these figures, there must always be an efficient political will, or, better yet, a political decision of transformation that is adapted to the social context.

In the practice of contemporary constitutional law, and in the literature it has produced, *constituent power is both recognized and excluded.* How can it be harnessed under the guise of a new figure of public—or rather, common—subjective rights that might allow for the development of a constitutional dynamics on par with the new realities of production and social constitution?

This question is the problem of democracy itself—the problem of its new definition as it passes into the postmodern.

We thus arrive at the new definition of the concept of democracy. For now, we shall limit ourselves to enumerating several elements of this definition, and we shall return to the question in greater depth in the following workshops.

First, we must distinguish *the concept of democracy as a "form of government,"* that is, as managing the unity of state and power, from the concept of democracy elaborated during the dark periods of modernity as "resistance" to the domination of an absolute state. Democracy appeared as *an absolute form of government*, that is, as a form of "government of all for all," or as a radical democratic form constructing the desire for freedom and equality from the base—always and everywhere. The socialist and communist movements of the nineteenth and twentieth centuries embraced this idea of democracy; it has been, and is still today, practiced by multitudinous movements. How can we then characterize the right to resistance (as an alternative and radical definition of public subjective law) faced with this idea—and this reality—of absolute democracy?

To conclude, we shall propose several considerations on the *concept of radical democracy.* In order to construct the latter, we must complexify traditional knowledge: insist on the difference between two conceptions of democracy. The first is a "form of government" that consists in the management of power and the articulation/exercise of the general will. The second is democracy as a project, as democratic praxis, as government "reform," that "exercises the common," and articulates the will of all.

If we want to refer to the ideological history of modernity in order to *grasp this ambivalence*, we must understand that there is, on the one hand, the great tradition of Western political thought, and on the other, the "mute history," the powerful non-history of materialism—a history of struggles and conquests, swept on and off by an ontological wager of great vitality (Machiavelli, Spinoza, and Marx interpreting the voices of the poor and the exploited). A "Dictionary of Communism" should be written to collect this mute history of struggles but also to translate the different languages of resistance and conflict through which it was given, this infinity of plural yet common histories. Something profoundly different, radically other, on the opposite spectrum of those enormous volumes of Marxist-Leninist history or of the history of the workers' movement that haunt our libraries... In sum: a new *Encyclopedia*...

Let us return for an instant to the problem at hand. We have at our disposal a series of phenomena, concepts, and movements to transform the "mute history" into an explicit "becoming multitude." On the one hand, we have *destructuring* (luttes déstructurantes) struggles: civil disobedience, sabotage, wage struggles that aim at destabilizing the productive structure, punctual struggles, conflictual relations with forms of command, etc., against democracy as a form of government. On the other, we have *constituent* struggles in favor of a democracy of the common, which develop autonomous forms of organization, collective self-management, a democratic exercise of the common, etc. *The relation between subjective rights and constituent power is determined at the heart this tension between "those who are against" and "those in favor."*

There is no need to emphasize up to what point these dynamics have been, and still are, experienced within the development of socialist and communist movements. However, it is probably useful to recall the harshness with which so-called "real socialism" neutralized and/or destroyed these movements. The fact is that "real socialism" belonged to modernity. On the contrary, in the transition towards the postmodern, we know that the concept of democracy as the exercise of the common can never again be assimilated to a form of government based on the categories of modernity.

When we analyze the concept of radical democracy, we must observe one last thing. Democratic movements, whether proletarian or, more generally, social, have always tried to resolve (contain, develop) democratic duality and contradiction into a linear process. There has always been a kind of linear model to sustain the development of struggles: linear, even when transition was conceived as violent laceration, as insurrectional rupture, and consequently, as a transitory form of dictatorship. *The question was, in all cases, to reunite democracy as a form of government and democracy as the exercise of the common. This tradition is no longer sustainable:* not only because of the impossibility of maintaining the continuity of the process, but because it is on this very continuity that the contradictions of globalized space are unleashed.

We must therefore consider something to which we shall return in greater depth in the following lessons and that we shall presently call the *democratic exodus.*

From a spatial point of view, if a democratic project (organized according to the will of all) exhibits a series of discontinuities and diversities that cannot be ascribed to a unity, the question is as follows: can an advanced democratic project develop on the global terrain of diversity? Here is an example. The concept of multitude—a class concept rooted in the hegemony of immaterial work—cannot exclude the mass movements of Chinese peasants, Brazilian struggles against biopower, Iranian or Indian antitheocratic insurgencies, etc. But then, what does it mean to take on this situation?

It is important, therefore, to bring the theme of cultural and corporal hybridization back on the table, specifically in political terms, as *a project capable of resolving the disjunctive dynamics of these differences on the material and historical terrain.* Only then might we be able to confirm the possibility of a process where discontinuity would drive new dynamics and novel political configurations. In this context, in turn, democratic exodus might propel the articulation and recomposition of multitudinous differences. There would be no teleology: just the experimentation of radical democracy that should subsume—and resolve—the discontinuities of a vast movement of ontological reclaiming. From the perspective of constituent power, democratic exodus would mean determining the new modes of ontological production of multitudinous subjects. *It is therefore clear that the theme of constitution must be taken up once again, radically, from the base.*

How can we construct *the will of all,* formally, juridically, and institutionally?

In the conception of democracy as a form of government, the construction of the general will is given through: 1) political representation and its transcendental reproduction; 2) the exercise of government, that is, the production of effective rules and norms; 3) the jurisprudential control of legitimacy and legality. This separation of powers dominates, and configures, the democratic system as a form of government.

We were asking ourselves how to juridically construct the will of all. This theme can in fact be articulated as follows: 1) how to determine new multitudinous forms of expression that might replace the transcendental function of political representation?; 2) how to construct efficient collective action within the common of life without falling back upon the characteristics of authority? How to ensure that it be the efficiency of constituent experience, that is, the efficiency of a majority action that is also consensual, driven by a will for transformation?; 3) How to implement a mechanism of self-control (*auto-contrôle*), both internal and external, in this open constitutional process?

Asking all these questions does not mean simply to renew certain initiatives of constitutional engineering. A constituent proposition can only construct a constitutional reality if it inserts itself critically—and creatively expresses itself—within a material and human web. We are dominated by an administrative, fiscal, and monetary system (the capitalist one), as well as by a repressive, media, and military system (again, the capitalist one): the rules of democracy as a form of government are tied to the functional rationality of these diverse agencies of domination. But it is clear that *democratic rules and the constitution of democracy, understood as the expression of the will of all, are unthinkable unless they radically transform this reality.* When we linked subjective rights to the right to resistance, we also linked subjective rights to the exercise of antagonism. This link is not some sort of undulatory relation that would alternate between resistance and antagonism. The space where transformation occurs is where subjective rights identify with the right to resistance. That is what exodus consists of.

When we spoke of resistance—on the one hand, the destructuring function of rupture, and on the other, constituent exercise as the management of the common—we did not exclude political violence. Even when the concept and practices of exodus are exasperated and brought to their extreme, we cannot completely exclude political violence. If we refer here to political violence, we are by no means theorizing it—neither as an instrument of struggle nor as an instrument of defense. Political violence is simply a function of democratic political action, because it exhibits resistance in its own way, and it imposes antagonism where the state can only affirm its domination and control. When the state-form of global capitalism is linked to war, then the relation between subjective law and the right to resistance inevitably becomes violent—precisely *against* war itself.

Workshop 8

Government and *Governance*: For a Critique of "Forms of Government"

In this workshop, we shall examine the possibility of a new definition of the concepts of government, governance, sovereignty, and Empire in order to constitute the base of a new political lexicon. Of course, through these definitions, we shall also implicitly try to define *the concepts of democracy and "absolute democracy"*—the first as a form of government of the One, the second as a form of the powerful, and not state-controlled, association of the multitude.

The distinction—or the division, to be exact—between democracy and "absolute democracy" is established by Spinoza not only in the *Political Treatise*, but also before that, in the last part of the *Ethics*. We cannot underestimate the importance of the Spinozan distinction: through this distinction, a long tradition of popular and multitudinous instances has consolidated in radical political terms—precisely those of "absolute democracy." We can already perceive in Machiavelli—and naturally justify through close readings—the birth of a concept of democracy that does not have much to do with the conceptual practice traditionally elaborated as "a form of government." We can find similar accents in the dramatic discussions accompanying the English revolution—contemporary to the development of Spinoza's thought. In reality, if we look carefully for premises of this line of thought, we encounter many instances of it—the currents of protestant sectarianism blowing through Europe after the end of the Renaissance, or, earlier still, the revolutionary Franciscanism following the way of a possible reform of church and state after the end of the Middle Ages.

It is not so much the history of the concept that interests us here, but rather the rupture that the notion of "absolute democracy," from Machiavelli and Spinoza, introduces in conceptions of the state, as well as the alternative it proposes.

The classical tradition has bequeathed us—in a hegemonic way, albeit with certain resistances—a theory of forms of government wherein democracy, and more generally the totality of the figures of power, was referred to the transcendent foundation of the One. In classical thought, forms of government are forms of the *management of the One*. Without this One, the state, power, and command cannot exist. The ambiguity of the Greek notion of *archè* lies precisely in its *simultaneous* definition of the principle and the command, of the genealogy and the legitimacy of government. Monarchy, aristocracy, and democracy are therefore nothing else than forms of management of the One. The Platonic *incipit* is followed by theorizations by thinkers such as Bodin or Hobbes; these rapidly become generalized in practices that legitimize power. For both, the classical legacy is fundamental, and the multitude cannot live within civil association and within the state unless it is first reduced to the One.

We are thus faced with a rather paradoxical phenomenon. It is the atheists and materialists—such as Bodin and Hobbes—that reintroduce transcendence, the foundation of the One, in order to guarantee all forms of power and all means of managing a collectivity, as well as the legitimizing power of all physical violence. A "One" in the shape of necessity.

Under these conditions, from Machiavelli to Spinoza, and through the sectarian currents of European Protestantism or pre-reform Franciscanism, the idea of democracy as *the government of all for all*, organized by free conflictuality, has become the absolute enemy of the state. The way in which we are today trying to define democracy is always the following: as the *government of each individual by each individual—but through all.*

Liberal-democrats have always kept their distance in relation to the traditional theories that define forms of government as the management of the One, and have often considered the classical definition of democracy as a mystification of pluralism. But in reality, what is constitutional bourgeois democracy if not a theory of the management of legitimate violence through the reduction of differences and complexity? Indeed, modern and contemporary politics have insisted beyond all measure on the following four ideas: there is no democracy that is not an *articulation of the One*; participation metamorphoses *the multitude into a people*; *separation of powers* is an instrument to guarantee its enactment; *political representation and legislation* are powers that participate in the One. The praise of nationhood has but confirmed this theoretical and practical arrangement, and has transformed it into myth.

As we shall see, the idea of the Republic, instead of criticizing the traditional conception of democracy, mystified its contents by transforming it (Rousseau exemplifies this) into a transcendental mediation of the general will in relation to the will of all. This was the very distinction that should have been explained and problematized, instead of it being reinforcing while feigning its invisibility!

It is interesting to note that in the twentieth century, when it came to understanding the nature of the state and not just referring to a historical point of view, the greatest theorists of constitutional sovereignty showed a complete lack of distinction between monarchy, aristocracy, and democracy. For Carl Schmitt, *state doctrine and constitutional theory are always—and only—an expression of political theology*. It is not surprising that dictatorship (or totalitarianism in late modernity) presents itself, albeit not as democratic, but as a function that remains constitutional. In its constitutional form, democracy is predisposed to cede to the state of exception: formal democracy bows down before the latter's implicit and intimate materiality. The constitutional political form of democracy is theorized as a function of the One and as a mystification of multiplicity.

Certain authors consider that the contemporary polemics around the definition of the concept of democracy demonstrate an extremely dangerous under-valuation of the power of law and institutions. It is clear that paying attention to the importance of juridical and institutional forms cannot disappear before the philosophical analysis of the conceptual knot constituted by democracy as a form of government. It is also true—as mentioned above—that, in our common usage of the term "democracy," our thought and our practice immediately imply the singular reappropriation of rights by the multitude.

Once this is said, we must nevertheless emphasize the dangers incurred by all conceptions of state—even democratic ones—and all theories of forms of government that are based on the idea of the One. In addition, there is no doubt that the *synthesis between the modern conception of the state and the mechanism of the nation* further complicated matters in that it hindered the possibility of a *soft*, continuous transition from the conception of democracy as a form of government to the exercise of democracy as a practice of the common.

It would now be interesting to examine the work of modern constitutional theorists in order to pose the problem, in the context we have just described, of the relation between law and figures of sovereignty. If it is true, in juridical theories of democracy, that the absolutism of the One is systematically interrupted by the emergence of the demands, instances, and institutions of the juridical subject, it is just as true that the state must continually render its own continuity effective and actualize its own genealogy by confronting both to the new surfacing of life, and making them coherent with the latter. Of course, this is even clearer if we place ourselves within a biopolitical horizon.

For the state, it seems, this can only end badly—like an ogre bound to keep devouring its own children. The state, even when it is democratic, possesses a sovereign continuity and coherence that is absolutely contradictory. Even if it is not managed in the manner of priests and ayatollahs, *neocons* or Stalinists, the absolute character of sovereignty is incessantly interrupted by social life, struggles, and the demands of singularities. *The right of exception* can no longer be thought of as a mechanism that prolongs the juridical organization of the state and the social organization of citizens, and that is tied to the simple brutality of power relations as if intervening *from the outside*. On the contrary, we are not speaking here of rupture. Rather, it is a continuous and coherent apparatus (*dispositif*) that intervenes from within the system (from within, albeit from the top) in order to block the spontaneity and the force of democratic movements. This apparatus is the more ferocious and pressing the more social communication and the maturity of labor have become organized within productive society. This is the paradox: the state of exception is the state's weakest element precisely because it is internal to its functioning. Even internal to sovereignty, the state of exception can never exhaust the vitality of resistances—and is therefore but an illusion.

When sovereign reality develops on a global scale, this analysis must be repeated and reinforced. Within globalized relations, *we no longer speak of the state of exception but of the state of war.* What we mean by war (let us clarify this so as not to fall prey to more or less subtly Hegelian misunderstandings) is not conflict *in general* but rather an asymmetrical war led by the strong against the weak. War interprets the state of exception by transforming it into a *global policing function*, that is, by insisting on that primary foundation of sovereignty: maintaining and reproducing order. The very principle of all this (the fact that *archè* signifies both legitimation and command, both peace and war) becomes itself global, and the concept of sovereignty glides over all the limits that the slow and difficult development of civilizations and struggles had imposed on war. Domination acquires the true measure of its power and a new extension of its effects through globalization. Its capacity to intervene in life is immediately intensified. *Henceforth, biopowers are asserted in/on/against the sphere of the biopolitical.* We had already noted this when we analyzed the efficiency of action of the nation-state; we must now simply enlarge our point of view to encompass globalization as a whole.

It is precisely at that moment, when the concept of sovereignty loses its outside and when transcendence imposes itself absolutely, that sovereignty can implode. The concept of resistance then reemerges against the principle of *archè*; it mingles with the concepts of freedom, of the secular (*la laïcité*), and cannot be suppressed.

We were just saying: it is at that very moment that *the concept of sovereignty might implode*. In fact, when the sovereign function represents itself as a state of exception and/or limitless war, then the sovereign concentrates within itself the maximal intensity of biopower. There are no elements left to encounter outside of its own power; there is no force that might feed its development. The concept of sovereignty implodes when it appears as exclusively transcendent; it excludes all possibility for life—a life that would not *already* be dominated—to pass through it. Here, we are not speaking of the death of life, but the life of death.

Careful: it is here that the concept of resistance acquires all its meaning, that it becomes synonymous with freedom and indistinguishable from the secular. We know that sovereignty can only be conceived in dualistic terms: when it is not reduced to the One, there are different forms that allow it to survive and develop. These are forms through which the strength and articulations of life and biopolitics nonetheless succeed in expressing themselves: although sometimes mystified, they remain efficient; although often unrecognized by the sovereign, they are obvious. When the principle of the One, of the *archè*, tries to impose itself not just conceptually but *really*—in which case it is a situation of war—sovereignty implodes.

The materialist philosophy of politics interprets the concept of sovereignty as both conflict and relation: the crisis of sovereignty is therefore both the crisis of this relation and a conflict that cannot be overcome. The discourse of materialist philosophy, however, is not simply grounded in moral ontology, in a series of judgments and second order consequences in relation to the disasters of power: it is a genuine epistemological reformulation of the approach to reality and truth. A materialist epistemology always has in mind the concrete relation that constructs truth: a relation through which the elements of experience are transformed into common notions and language. However, all this occurs without reality being negated or mystified, and the multiplicity of social relations is maintained and included in the pluralist context of the political management of the common. The dualistic epistemology of materialism, able to recognize the enemy and distinguish the One from the multiple, must be proposed anew as an essential condition in the political field so that a new pluralist ordering can be defined.

The crisis of sovereignty becomes most explicit when, *in modern theory* and, following that, in Empire, government becomes the fundamental—and single—element in the management of power and when the concept of democracy is entirely subordinate to the maintenance and reproduction of a unilateral exercise of power (that is, in its most dramatic form, in the nationalisms and colonialisms of the modern period).

This crisis is not a theoretical affirmation but a practical experience: in fact, *the effectiveness of a diffuse and irresistible resistance corresponds to the crisis of legitimacy.* There are many ways to describe this resistance: from the refusal of politics and abstention from politics, to the crisis of political representation, the explosion of social relations or the decline of economic systems... What is even more interesting is that, faced with the clear crisis of the traditional modern government, we can now use the theme of *governance.*

What is *governance*? It is the attempt to inscribe social conflicts and administrative procedures within the specific, punctual, and singular mediations of sovereign power. We are not trying to erase the very real newness and rupture of *governance* in relation to the tradition of modern government. Nor are we trying to reduce it simply to a postmodern version of *Raison d'Etat* or *Polizeiwissenschaft*. What we would like to do, on the contrary, is *show, through the pragmatics of governance, the element of crisis that will allow us to affirm the disappearance of the traditional definition of government.*

Let us return, for example, to a discourse we have already developed theoretically and that we must reformulate from a historical point of view. "Republicanism" asserted itself as a fundamental tendency of government at the same time as constitutionalism, and parallel to it, at the end of the three great bourgeois revolutions. It represented the ideological version—that would be theorized by Kant under the form of a transcendentalism—of a constitutional politics and practice meant to resolve the contradictions of society, sovereignty and the temporality of political action *on the field of the One.* At the end of the eighteenth century, republicanism was already a pragmatics of governance—founded, it is true, on political representation and social mediation rather than on conflicts, difficulties of administrative relations, and the class struggle, as is the case today. But once these differences are recognized, the fact remains that *recourse to the pragmatics of governance will always involve the hegemony of government.* The paradox we emphasized above—that the autonomous development of law can never succeed in modifying forms of government—is once again verified.

This critique of republicanism holds true for the continental juridical tradition that found its highest expression in German thought on public law—and in Kelsenian formalism. It also holds true for all the variations on traditional juridical-publicist themes in Anglo-Saxon law at a time when the jurisprudential production of law was considered the means of configuring, or sustaining a communitarian reality. Communitarianism—a classical notion in Anglo-American theories of law production—organically reproduces the belief and faith in the continuity of the state: the inductive line that communitarianism follows is thus *formally*, and not *materially*, opposed to the deductive dynamics that are, on the contrary, typical of continental thought. Kelsen himself, in his later work, showed this contiguity well.

In this context, what can a definition of the absolute democracy of the multitude signify? Does this definition consist in a pure and simple—and violent—reversal of the theoretical framework we have been exposing? Or, on the contrary, must this definition take into account the modifications of the conditions in which practices of government and of *governance* are developing today? In particular, can we record—and at the same time reverse—the dynamics of *governance* so that the proposal for absolute democracy might emerge at the heart of this reversal? In sum: is absolute democracy born inside the crisis of modern sovereignty?

In reality, absolute democracy is not the definition of a new "form of government." On this point, we absolutely agree with most exegetes of "alternative" and revolutionary thought from the modern period. Machiavelli, Spinoza, or Marx gave no other definition of democracy than that of absolute democracy, and they conceived of it only through the field of singularities and the multiplicity. Absolute democracy inevitably—and essentially—presents itself as a production of subjectivity that is both singular and multitudinous. The absolute characteristic of democracy determines itself based on the incapacity of the One to conserve the multiple. There is no metaphysical presupposition in this, no mystery, no enigma of power, no delegation of *potentia* (puissance), no presupposed community, etc. However, this does not mean that the multiple cannot become active and efficient, that it cannot construct apparatuses adapted to its own existence—never *a priori*, always in the heat of action—in a process that is the process of human *action* itself. Here, biopolitics appears as the real terrain of politics, its essential condition. Rather than an absolute concept, we should instead speak of an "absolute pragmatics" of democratic expression.

How do we then redefine sovereignty—all the while knowing that this redefinition implies not only conceptual work but also understanding the new reality that immediately corresponds to it? What might "sovereignty" mean if the modern concept that corresponds to it is in crisis, and if, in the postmodern period, the alternative of absolute democracy is what is on the horizon? Today, we can speak of sovereignty only as a crisis within a relation of forces that necessarily includes power relations and constituent *potentias*.

Saying this—with the advent of the postmodern—we are grasping *the core of the Machiavellian analysis of power*. It is a relation of power, of course, but mostly a double intention: *on the one hand, to acknowledge the enemy, on the other, to constitute the common*. Thinking back on the history of the crisis of the modern concept of sovereignty, we remain circumscribed to a field that pinpoints the incapacity of either pole—capital, or the sovereign bourgeois state—to govern. But it is absolutely insufficient to speak only of a crisis of sovereignty. Every counter-conduct, action of resistance, or alternative proposal not only contests power but also expresses the common. *Resistance is a construction.* Today, this constructive capacity, that of a power that has been historically reversed in favor of the multitude, must necessarily affect the concept of sovereignty.

Careful: our affirmations here also concern certain interpretations of Marx—whether from within Marxism, or against it. These interpretations insist on reducing resistance to the expression of a force. According to us, it is not simply the expression of a *force*, but the expression of a *power* (puissance)—and this is absolutely different: not only destruction, but also reconstruction, innovation, project. Of course, in Marx and in certain Marxist readings, the isolation of the concept of *Gewalt* (and the violence of its use) has sometimes been extreme. Yet what interests us is another aspect of the expression of resistance. What is most important is to register the caesura between the modern and the postmodern as an ontological rupture, a genuine leap of intensity, the transformation of the project of subjects acting within history. Our hypothesis is the following: *multitudinous subjectivity determines hegemonic effects.* The caesura between the modern and the postmodern is not simply a passing moment in history. It is a moment in which subjects and their hegemonic relations are transfigured in a given historical context: hegemony, today, is the multitude.

In this situation, how can we define the notion of *government*? We can only understand it as a *decision*, within a contradictory multiplicity that cannot be collected under any "schema of Reason." Government is no longer a form of power. It is increasingly *a space* wherein *potentias* of the common confront themselves. It would be useful here to recall the criticism we directed at all the transcendental/republican mediations in theories of government.

There is, however, a knot that seems to hinder our analysis: the difficulty of explaining the passage from the crisis of capitalist government (faced with forces of resistance) to the capacity of decision as an expression of the common. This relation is far from being resolved, yet it seems to represent the essential context wherein we can critique forms of government—in the transitory phase we are going through. From the point of view of the forces of resistance and of the common, we must now start debating the possibility of another apparatus of government: a theory, a capacity…

In reality, all these problems refer to the definition of what is meant by "decision" today and how *this "decision" relates to the common. They also call for a new elaboration of political anthropology in this specific framework.* We shall return to this in the next workshop.

We had started with the notion of *governance* and its meaning in the context of the crisis of sovereignty, faced with the parallel emergence of instances of absolute democracy. Today, we can only define it as the absolutely necessary transition towards the exercise of constituent power (or more exactly: constituent *potentia*). This means that governance must lead to the possibility of a *vis democratica* that would be born from the base, from multiplicity, through the construction of a common *potentia. Consequently, we must simply invert the traditional idea of governance after having broken its internal mechanism*—a mechanism that always brought decision back to the mediation between state necessity and the particularity of individual demands. On the contrary, it seems that the concept of *governance* must be established totally—and with no exception—*according to a pragmatics of the exercise of the common.*

We cannot give examples of this reorientation of *governance* without referring to *multilevel* juridical categories whose (often ambiguous) effects always determine jurisprudential apparatuses that are very innovative in regards to the modern tradition of the relation between sovereignty and law. As you must know, in contemporary jurisprudence, *multilevel* signifies the acknowledgment of the multiplicity of sources of law and of juridical rules that are efficient conjointly.

We recently insisted upon the fact that, one way or another, the law is always absorbed by a kind of whirlwind of sovereignty. Now, based on the ambiguity of the relations above, we wish to emphasize up to what point these processes can also reveal absolute democratic *potentias*.

Yet we arrive at no genuine conclusion. This is also because *multilevel* juridical categories refer not only to singular demands (always understood as exercises of the common) and to actual state responses, but also to processes of constituting institutions, that is, to the common sediment of constituent experience and the capacity to interrupt and renew it at any moment. Claims to *Multilevel* management are ineffective as long as they remain under the power of the One and have not found another source of genuine democratic legitimacy—the will of all for all.

One last question. In light of all these elements, how can we also redefine what we call Empire? We must, perhaps, dare to be sectarian and slightly utopian: Empire is the only spatiotemporal, ethical, ontological, political, and economic dimension wherein the multitude might engage in a practical experimentation of freedom. We must, however, remember that when we speak of Empire, we are speaking of a tendency characterized by a strong crisis: it is an *interregnum* during which a subversive and revolutionary state of fact had been affirmed in a decisive manner. By definition, a tendency is always exposed to all the risks, ebbings, and suspensions to which we have become accustomed through the historical development of struggles. *There is nothing teleological in the process of history.* However, when social, political, and biopolitical relations have arrived at such a degree of antagonism, that process *is no longer reversible.* This means that old forms of sovereignty cannot be restored.

Let us conclude. The *theory* of "forms of government" that is rooted in the classical tradition disappears once the *practice* of government descends into crisis. This crisis corresponds to the impossibility of recomposing, through a constant mechanism of transcendental unification, the contradictory determinations of social relations and class relations into institutional forms penetrated by the action of the multitudes. Replacing the authoritarian mechanisms of government by the mediation procedures of *governance*—that have been introduced to resolve the difficulties encountered by the government—increases, deepens, and probably renders the crisis of government irreversible, including in the modern exceptionality of its definition. Consequently, it is within the context of *governance* that the class struggle led by the multitudes must be developed.

Workshop 9

Decision and Organization

For us, singularity is both difference and resistance, and the multitude is a collection of singularities. As we have seen, difference signifies, above all, an excess, an invention, a construction—the positive construction of new values.

Yet is it clear that, in practice, singularity is not always equivalent to this excess. Excess is an eventuality, whereas the relation between singularities is, on the contrary, very often both ontologically and politically normalized. Since classical atomism, many authors have insisted upon the fact that resistance is a virtual possibility, sometimes an improbable virtuality. Excess is consequently a structurally indeterminate event, a fact that can appear in complete indifference, an innovative relation that is absolutely without finality and/or precise cause. The fact that singularities exist does not automatically mean that they will be able to construct difference, that is, to posit themselves as resistant.

Once we take this situation under consideration, and once we recognize the haphazard character of such passages into resistance, *it is nonetheless necessary to return to the specific problem of difference as excess.*

In particular, we must remember that difference is brought about—produced, realized—by a series of relations that exist between resistant singularities that, by continuously integrating other relations and other elements, end up forming what we have called a *"network,"* a *"Web" of cooperation*. The finality of this cooperation is not to produce excess. Its finality, and its primary condition, is rather to *express meaning*. But when we express meaning *as excess*, when, therefore, "expression is produced," we invest existence and innovate on the terrain of being. We must therefore analyze excess as the production of meaning, expression, surplus—as the production of subjectivity. We shall return to all of this once we deal with the other problem that is still hanging in the air, the question of *decision*.

Let us look at *the problem of the way we construct decision based on difference*. Many have wondered about the relation between the multitude and the One (inasmuch as it seems that decision cannot be anything else than this One: a unitary and unilateral decision). The concept of multitude is considered a phenomenologically correct idea yet one that is politically indecisive: how can the multitude—this multiplicity of differences, whose genesis cares not for identity and arithmetic unity—transform into a political subjectivity and become powerful in the decision and the execution of command?

From a functional point of view, this objection grows even stronger if we consider the problem qualitatively. How, and in what way, can the multitude present itself as an antisystemic power? What can provide a place for it within the real contradictions that characterize the world, development, and the constitution of power? Of course, we answer such questions by maintaining that *resistance's excess and the production of subjectivity expressed by singularities advance on the traces of the common*. But, supposing this is true, *how can we construct decision—and common decision—based on differences?*

In order to answer such questions, we must establish, and describe, areas and spaces in which we might intervene conceptually and practically. These spaces are at the same time spaces of thought and spaces nourished by experience: it is from them that we must proceed.

Let us start with the question—oh how difficult—of the time and structure of decision. What do we mean by decision? The act of an individual will? Certainly not. Machiavelli, and more generally, all those who have analyzed political decision, because they viewed decision in its singularity, inferred that the model of individual decision was insufficient. *The singular decision is, on the contrary, an act of will that implies infinite determinations.* It is not a kind of sword that man might maneuver at will, but rather a huge machine that only common realities can manage. Only these common realities *can decide.*

Decision is thus a common act. How should we understand such an affirmation? Should we understand: the will of the masses, the hegemony of the avant-garde, the capacity of representative instances to become a singular body, etc.? The problem is, in reality, always that of the concentration of a will—in this case not individual but common—that is and remains singular and productive.

There are certain essentially anarchist currents of thought (born before socialism, and probably derived from radical Anabaptism or Franciscanism) that metaphysically negate the possibility that decision might be genealogically collective and teleologically common. By metaphysical negation, these movements refer to an impossibility taken as absolute, linked to human nature, or possibly to the theological imperfection of individuals. Our hypothesis is the opposite; it considers difference, resistance, singularity and the common as linked among themselves in a continuous game of construction and ontological innovation. *Lived experience characterizes itself on that terrain: that is where it qualifies, articulates, and decides itself.*

But once this premise is accepted, the problem still remains open. The fact that conditions of radical and revolutionary innovation can manifest through a certain number of processes of decision does not automatically imply that these conditions are immediately recognizable and materially reproducible as *potentias* of the multitude.

We should therefore further examine the ontological dimensions of decision (in this case, essentially temporal), and attempt to define them not as *the will of the One* but as *the expression of the multitude*. This is the knot we must untie in order to be able to return to political processes. What do we understand by "decision" once it is defined as the expression of a multitude and inserted in a *telos* (*a posteriori*) of the movements of the *common*, in a project of common action?

Before advancing further in that direction, let us review *four points* that will be useful to our reasoning, since they all touch upon the problem of the relation between singularity, difference, and the common.

There is a *first problem* that has been known since the beginning of time, and that has not lost any of its acuity: it is the conflictual relation between a natural conception of difference, and a cultural and historical one. It was only in the twentieth century that philosophical critique and feminist analyses, concerning a notion that historicism had always tried to elucidate, showed that overcoming this antithesis did not open onto the universal, and did not reproduce any dialectical process. This advance towards difference was, on the contrary, a trajectory driven towards acknowledging the common. The absolute affirmation of difference (natural or cultural) was in fact an epistemological and ontological progression that tried to construct real expressions of difference radically excluding all forms of identity. This search for the common is often what we have chosen to call, following Spinoza, "*moving towards a common name.*"

But what does moving towards a common name mean? What are the theories and constructions of the common name? The practices of this construction consider the process of cooperation between singularities as ontologically expressive and temporally open. In this context, the present can only be read from the point of view of the future, that is, according to an immersion into the present that contains in itself the tendency towards the future. It is within this framework that the common produces. In this interplay of jumps and rebounds between past and future, subjectivity can never be stuck in one identity, whatever that may be. At that point, what we might call the "materialist landings of the common" become visible: the oscillation between the objective and the subjective, where they convergence and even become shared—and, in reality, where their old phenomenological distinction is overcome. In this perspective, the common becomes the fundamental condition of cooperation and resistance. We shall consider excess and decision on precisely that terrain. *Indeed, the common appears not only as a result but also as a condition—a virtual condition transposed into the regime of real possibility.*

Consequently, we have a first element that will allow us to approach the theme of decision: natural difference and cultural difference do not advance towards the universal; on the contrary, they regenerate singularities in the common.

Of course, this is far from being enough. Moving from our first difficulty—that of understanding if difference could determine a common decision—and deciding to renew our bets and affirm that difference can express itself outside of separation and identity, that is, as *a common creative element*, means that we inevitably return to the dynamic apparatuses of difference and the common. We must, therefore, ontologize the problem, and wonder which expressions of being might sum up the processes leading from the multitude (differences, resistance) to (common) decision.

And so we turn our attention to the question of the *event*, namely, *the analysis (the acknowledgment) of how the multitude of differences and singularities presents itself before the emptiness of decision*. The emptiness of the common decision is an emptiness of being; it is an absolute deficit. Nothing can save us from the fact that this emptiness can sometimes be interiorized by the multitude. When this happens to philosophy, it leads to negative thought. When it happens to existence, it submerges us in a world of sad passions. But there are so many perceptions, sentiments, experiences and concepts that tell us, on the contrary, that this emptiness exhorts us to defy it, to fill it up, to throw weak bridges into its abyss. In sum: to decide about decision. Waiting for an event that might allow this power (*puissance*) to express itself becomes intolerable when it is accompanied by inertia. In any case, it is unequivocal. It is the most important sign of this phase of crisis.

The *second fundamental trait* of this waiting on decision is the presence of specific determinations that are not always clear in the contradictory context in which they appear. This trait emerges, for example, on the superficial level of subjectivities. It appears in boredom, disorder, quarrels, in all the background noise surrounding us, or in the weight of repressive tendencies on the most ordinary daily life. In order to get out of this situation, philosophers try to detect a hegemonic figure that might reverse this dispersion effect of indeterminate appearance. We shall return to this shortly. But what we wish to do here is emphasize the objective tension created between these determinations, difficult to detect, and the search for hegemony, and insist upon waiting for the event. This event wants to be hegemonic. However, against the entire tradition of political thought, its hegemony also wants to be common.

Third point: up to now, we have insisted on the common. But what does it mean to *subjectivate* the common? Or, more exactly: how can we return a subjective depth to the common that is generally forgotten? Acknowledging the problem of decision can, of course, neither be individual nor collective. It remains, however, singular, precisely because it is common. Let us be clear. We really do not know what to do with the individual demons of the great criminals of history—or with collective demons, when these have existed. These poor objects of historical thought too often correspond to mystifications produced by certain idealistic and quite unhistorical rereadings of history. Of course, we are not denying the horror of Hitler or Stalin; rather we are saying that the problem of decision cannot be reduced to the acknowledgment of their monstrosity. If the presence of the individual in history and its weight therein constitutes a problem, it cannot be resolved without closely linking, on the one hand, subjectivation, historical conditions, singularities, and differences, and on the other, the reasons of the common. *We must therefore establish a terrain that might represent a genuine entelechy of subjectivity and the common,* in other words, that will enable us to understand how the historical assemblage (*agencement*) of the common is phenomenologically determined. The space in which to discuss the problem of decision is specified later.

Fourth point: we must consider *the problem of organization* in relation to the theme of decision that we are examining. Contrary to what is often thought, the theme of organization can be considered internal to decision—something we are not denying in the least—as well as external to it. When organization is based in the collective common, and constructed from the expression of the singular resistances that the common generates, the will to organization—as all will to power—can be a variable independent of all the historical determinations of political decision. For example, it is not true that organization cannot exist outside of the traditional forms of collective decision such as parties or political representation. Conversely, parties and forms of political representation have sometimes succeeded in passing beyond the level of collective decision into that of common decision. They have then appeared as genuine constituent powers. In all cases, however, this remained a variable. *Common decision is always a free intervention, a genuine clinamen.*

On the basis of these four points, let us take up the analysis of the modalities of decision once again, that is to say, more generally, the modalities of its ontological dimensions.

According to us, this is an absolutely fundamental theme. It opposes the "internal limit" of the tension of singularities towards the common to its "external limit." This external limit corresponds to the obstacle that the internal initiative of subjectivity encounters when it wishes to produce the event, when it exposes itself above the emptiness of being and takes the risk of, or bets on, *kairòs*. It is important to understand that decision shall be the more open and exposed on its external limit—almost to an extreme limit—the more it is fed by common labor and by the "ontological deposits" of this production. This opening is of course *a risk*, but is also *a power* (puissance).

What then seems particularly interesting to analyze—and eventually to reformulate in sociological terms in order to reinvest it in political action—is the way the multitude's dangerous approach to the event constructs positive forces, novel qualitative characterizations, and new cooperative tensions. In sum, posing the problem of the event in the decision of the multitude—by means of the relation between singularities and the common—we find the strong presence of obstacles and repression, of elements of blockage and fatigue. And yet, this situation of conflict can paradoxically *redetermine ontological functions of innovation*—both in relation to the composition of the multitude (and consequently to the source and the form of decision) and in relation to the real dynamics of the movement (and therefore to the possibility of determining the event itself).

Let us say a few words about the material conditions of this process. *If there is an effective entelechy between the subjective and the common, clearly, this materiality is absolutely essential,* and the point is fundamental. As things stand, the material presupposition to which we must refer is that of *the new figure of capital.* Now, in post-Fordist capitalism, the action of subjectivity—that represents itself from the materialist point of view as "cognitive labor"—does not have any function as "variable capital." We know that, in the Marxian theory of capital, variable capital is held in the meshes of total/constant capital. Yet living and cognitive labor no longer corresponds to it. The metamorphosis of capitalism gives rise to new interpretative categories as well as new realities. Regardless of the proposed interpretations of this novel situation, it seems that they all provide a new qualification of "real subsumption:" when this subsumption is realized, when it executes the passage from the modern to the postmodern (or from Fordism to post-Fordism), then the labor force becomes relatively autonomous in relation to capitalist power and to its accumulation. Subjects' *autonomy* is paradoxically given "within" the real subsumption of society under capital. In other words, this autonomy presents itself as virtually independent of processes of capitalist accumulation. New "use values" are emerging where "exchange value" had previously imposed its absolute hegemony. The capitalist dictatorship is interrupted—in relation to investments as well as to consumption: the measurelessness (*démesure*) of accumulation must confront an excess/autonomy of living work that throws the frame of capitalist subsumption completely off balance. *Consequently, we must oppose a transversal vision to all unilateral and monocratic conceptions of capitalist development.* The context of capitalist development is a social context that functions as a background against which the power (*puissance*) of living labor stands out.

We can now formulate a small—and incomplete—conclusion to the problem of the temporal and ontological source of decision. Once posited the above conditions, the question becomes that of the passage (*or transmutation*) from *potentia* to *decision*, in other words, the way in which we render cooperative networks vertical, and how we develop a common expression of the common. *This verticalization is never a hierarchy, and it maintains the totality of* potentia.

We have until now tried to present certain essential conditions for a "decisive" intervention on the problem of decision. These conditions, as we have seen, move between difference and singularity as biopolitical desire, bodily apparatuses, or rational determinations. To be more correct, we should invoke instead the cooperation between these three aspects. The affirmation of the common plays upon these three elements and finds its moment of verification through decision. We have already developed the issues of the power (*puissance*) of existing groups, of their constituent tension, of the qualified and articulated expression of the multitude. Our analysis must now continue around the frameworks of biopolitical desire, the bodily apparatus of being and the rational determination of decision.

It is not only a question of understanding what decision signifies, but also of understanding what a democratic decision signifies.

Before confronting the problem of democratic decision, let us take an argumentative detour through a series of problems connected to organization.

When we speak of organization, we often refer to it as an institution, namely, as a condition that is instituted rather than constituent. What is the difference between the two terms? In reality, the distinction is hard to pinpoint from our position, since we are immediately faced with an obvious paradox. *Potentia* and constituent power must always pass through institutions. They must belong to the coherence of the latter, to the continuity of the operative system that organizes them. At least, this is what constitutional theory rather realistically affirms. Yet institutions have often, if not always, been separated from ways of life. This means that they are, consequently, separated from the action of *potentia* or from what we call constituent power. How can we think of a constituent power that passes through the institution without presenting itself as teleology, without necessarily flattening the projections and jumps of its own movement? Finally: how do we take charge of this institutionalizing process efficiently?

When we try to confront this series of problems, we are on *ontological terrain*. When we try to follow the development of a possible materialist teleology, we presuppose, in particular, a material continuity in the development of struggles and instances of liberation, a projection of bodies and an active expression of the biopolitical. All of these elements have not been properly defined, even though Foucault and many Foucauldians worked at giving them a genuine conceptual consistency: we shall return to this shortly.

However, through this novel problematization, we also run the risk of the *insurgence of the negative*. When we construct a direct line, through the real dynamics of movements, from decision to organization, we are always blocked by the objection—philosophical but also real—according to which this process can never be totally disengaged from the weight of negativity. For certain critics, the insistence on negativity is so strong that it masks the positivity of the process of constituting organization. In this case, this negativity is not the one we find in Hegel, namely, a *reactionary negativity* that relativizes the effects of the positive. Instead, this negativity

presents the effects of the positive as incomprehensible and powerless: we are thinking, of course, of Heideggerian negativity.
Why are huge philosophical machineries of the sort still produced
and used to repress the most original and fruitful trajectories of
resistance and hope? The only justification seems to be that issues
of organization and institutionalization are flattened upon those
of resistance and legitimization. We find everything that is
objective, odious.

Today, certain positions try to uphold, in terms of the critique
of the teleological-materialist link, a series of arguments asserting
their kinship with Foucault. Of course, we are not inspired by the
same Foucault. These positions propose "counter-behaviors" that
are supposed to found the possibility of all new institutional
processes. Yet these counter-behaviors are nothing else than
"counter-powers;" rather than threaten power, they reproduce it in
an inverted form. They are its *symmetrical and inverse doubles*, and
remain on an institutional level. They never position themselves on
the terrain of constituent *potentia*. We think they are just as odious
as the processes of objectivation we were just referring to.

On the contrary, *materialist teleology is a productive force and
a* potentia *that recomposes, synthetically and conclusively, all the
elements that constitute the reality of historical processes*. In this context, the referral to negativity is no doubt important, but it
should not become reactionary. The problem is not to exclude the
negative but to construct the positive—both lines are always
crisscrossing.

Against all the analyses mentioned above, we believe that institutions can be different than capitalist ones. They must be invented
by constituent power itself, and must represent its first element of
multitudinous organization. The problem at hand is therefore the

continuity and the means of the organization of action, the *praxis* of the multitude.

And thus, once again, we ask: *what is a decision?*

We have already stated that organization should be understood as two things. On the one hand, it is the positive, material and innovative capacity to build—a capacity that insists on the onto-logical dimensions of the process of transformation and affirms its hold there. On the other, simultaneous to the opening of orga-nization towards the future, it is the capacity to destroy and to deny everything that diffuses death and asphyxiates the old world. It is in the midst of this extremely violent dynamics that decision and organization are affirmed. No teleologically efficient decision exists that has not come from resistance, from an exodus from all the forces (organizations and institutions) that were blocking the development of *potentia*. Power and *potentia*, biopowers and biopolitical forces are elements confronting each other in today's period of transition from one world to another, from one civilization to another. Of course, by civilization we never mean to refer to an identity but to a collection of historically and spatially determined structures.

The space of decision—and consequently the grounding of possible organization—is not a problem that can be defined, or limited to either partial or global physical space. On the contrary, decision and organization appear in the relation that exists between the different forces simultaneously passing through global and local spaces. When we speak of organization (that is, an essential transmutation of movements and institutions—inas-much as organization always comes out of the exercise of a counter-power, not continuing it but *going beyond it*), or when we speak of the organization of the multitudes, we mean the possibility of expressing a general point of view, integrated into local decisions, which, through them and for them, becomes a common name and a common decision.

From this perspective, one of the most important problems that movements must confront is *overcoming all experiences of counter-power, in the strict meaning of the term.* In counter-power, the homology between the resistance exerted by movements and the dominant power from which this resistance tried to distinguish itself was pushed to its limit. We know that there can be no genuine expression of resistance without emphasizing the constitutive, alternative and subversive element of transformation, as well as *the ontological difference* between power and *potentia.* There is no doubt that we owe the maturity of today's movements to the clear consciousness of this essential point.

Based on all these elements, we can now formulate a new definition of the concept of "revolution." Our hypothesis is as follows: revolution is an acceleration of historical time, the realization of a subjective condition, an event, an opening, all of which concur to make the production of an irreducible and radical subjectivity possible. The problem of decision is therefore resolved within this framework.

Yet we must also address the material condition in which the production of subjectivity is rooted. This condition can be characterized as the emergence of a new potential of desire and productivity in a given historical moment.

In order to pursue this investigation—and decipher what corresponds to this condition today—we must insist on the appearance of the new potential represented by the new productive labor force and the autonomy of the multitude. This potential is a social capital represented by today's forms of capitalist accumulation and order, as well as by the new use values that correspond to the autonomy of living work. It is based on this potential that *novel contradictions* emerge—material, certainly, but also subjective. Yet, whereas subjective contradictions are active, material contradictions are essentially found in repressive terms, since capital cannot detach from the parasitical dimensions that characterize it. The new use values expressed through the autonomy of living work seem to contain a theoretical schema and/or a practical tendency that very well might bring us to a genuine revolutionary moment.

To shed light on this point, it might be useful to take into account *a certain typology of revolutionary events*. We are thinking of four revolutionary experiences: the English, French, Russian and American revolutions.

What we wish to emphasize in the French Revolution is how perfectly the schema we have constructed above functions. The French Revolution exhibits a decision that is produced precisely from the new consistency of social capital. This capital arises at the end of the first period of bourgeois accumulation and, through the deepest contradictions, produces a form of constitutional organization that corresponds to it. The French Revolution is thus subject to the historical consistency of accumulated capital and to the subversive insistence of the new social forces that are liberated at the time. Except for a temporal difference, the same could be said of the English Revolution.

In Russia, these conditions are pushed to their limit by the extreme tension that social relations liberate, as these are compressed by the imperialist war. In the Russian Revolution, the material conditions are fundamental inasmuch as they violently affirm the limits of living a revolutionary adventure and finding a constitutional equilibrium.

As an aside, we might mention Hannah Arendt's complete misunderstanding of the Russian Revolution, even after her equivocal mumblings in favor of "Rosa Luxemburg type" advice. She does not understand that *it is impossible to distinguish between a social and a political revolution*, and that the Russian Revolution, even though it is desperate, is a revolution that is quite capable of expressing the ontological power (*puissance*) of humanity. If a situation can illustrate the concept of decision, it is this one: the goal of our argument is to *affirm decision based on the essential continuity between the social and the political.*

The outline we have used up to now concerning continental revolutions can equally be applied to the revolution and the constitutional process that constructed the United States of America—with certain differences in relation to which it might be useful to invoke Hannah Arendt, critically of course. Hannah Arendt maintains that the American Revolution is not social but political, and that it does not concern the foundations of property but instead organizes public space.

We admit that we have never been able to understand why this misinterpretation has become commonplace in political philosophy. Such a misinterpretation seems quite crude. A quick, yet efficient, analysis might easily show that the American Revolution (and the construction of American institutions) only ends after the Civil War, and on the premise of two fundamental decisions: on the one hand, the abolition of slavery and the consequent generalization of the capitalist mode of production, on the other, the new subdivision of continental space (along with the genocide of Native American populations) in favor of the Northern industrial states. We are a long way from the formal democracy dear to Hannah Arendt, and the constitution of a public space... *On the other hand, we are in the center of social decision, in other words, at the heart of politics.*

The Time of Common Freedom

"The Time of Common Freedom": we could just as well have given this last workshop the title "Alternatives provided by Common Freedom," or, simpler yet, "Of Common Freedom." What interests us foremost is the argument that affirms that *becoming a multitude means to immediately produce democracy*. We shall see in particular that the task of constituting the multiple and democracy is one that must be chosen: a goal to attain, an ethical and political apparatus to realize.

In the preceding workshop, we analyzed the form of the passage from decision to organization. We then defined the conditions of the passage from organization to the transformation of political reality, that is, to the realization of the common according to the needs of a materialist teleology for which there is no *telos* before action. It is useful to insist on the specific content of this double passage.

When we say that democracy is a revolution, we are not speaking of democracy as a form of government but of democracy as civil life, or as the emergence—from the base—of *claims* and projects, redistributions and decisions. We must therefore increase our understanding of the content of the democratic process, identify the common *telos* it produces, and the tendencies it projects. The theme of common freedom here runs parallel to *the temporality* of this freedom: the production of the multitude and of democracy finds an essential matrix in this open temporality.

In order to understand the theme of common freedom, or better yet, *the temporality of common freedom*, our reasoning shall develop according to ontologically determined stages and shall follow a number of historically defined *deadlines*. Such deadlines are the limits of the periodizations we are establishing. As we shall see, they relate essentially to the production of political subjectivities, as well as to the dynamics of passions and the communities that intersect with their composition. They also relate to the different forms in which the exercise of the common confronts the exercise of power.

It is important to emphasize that the production of a political subjectivity is given as a *body*. This means that political subjectivity cannot exist without the continuous renewal of passions, projects, and constructions of new "artificial" facts—artificial because they are always reinvented—that characterize and constitutionalize common life. Political subjectivity appears as a body because it is *a permanent metamorphosis of bodies*: it is a *doing*.

When we say that the body is implied, in an essential way, in the process of construction of political subjectivities, we are saying something that is less clear than it might appear. Both the subjectivity that becomes a political body and the body that becomes a political subjectivity are immersed in the progression of becoming-multitude (*faire*-multitude). We must be very careful: this relation between a political subjectivity and a singular body (in other words, this new way of considering the relation between singularity and multitude) appears in the political debate—and in political theory—*around 1968*. This "body" has nothing to do with the different metaphors of the social or political body haunting modern political thought. What unites the "bodies" we are speaking of is no longer the general will considered as an organic body but *the flesh of singular bodies—as singular—in the multitude*. This new field of discussion has completely renewed the context and the terms of political analysis. Once again, we therefore verify the consistency of the postmodern caesura.

Once the historical conditions of this process are clarified, it seems useful to insist on the issue of discontinuity and *on what we might call the "doubling" of subjectivity as it becomes political*. If subjectivity appears as a determined ontological condition (being-proletarian, being-woman, being-worker, etc.), it can also present itself as the voluntary decision to constitute itself as a force (resistance, power, war). The temporary discontinuity of cycles of struggles and the increase of fields of reference of political consciousness mix and interconnect according to diagrams that are always different. We analyzed above the process of gaining political consciousness—the expression is awful, please be indulgent towards this all too Sartrian expression!—through the difference of potential of social conflict. By potentials of social conflict, we mean the antagonistic tensions that subsist in the gap *between the "technical" and the political composition of the multitude*, or between the different forms of political control that try to manage this gap. We must now refer this discontinuity to the differences, both concrete and political, of *subjective doubling*. In other words, we must understand how the gaps we have been speaking of are experienced, felt and acted upon by singular subjectivities.

Second element: when we speak of subjectivities, we must pinpoint the emergence of the common and its acknowledgment. By this, we mean the process through which we go from the multiplicity of singularities to their complex representation as a political force. Clearly, we must consider this process from the point of view of a temporal discontinuity, according to the cycles of different political behaviors. We must also consider it according to the doubling of subjective bodies, doubling that functions as a reflection within the constituent process and as the key to its construction.

Finally, when we speak of the "common" or of the "constitution of the common," we must emphasize the fact that the common is always omniversatile, *it is always a multiplicity*, a complexity, a collection of subjectivities. The production of subjectivities always passes through the multiple, neither excluding nor canceling it. On the contrary, this production develops the multiple through the relations it establishes, as it constructs common behaviors and languages. We might note here the parallelism that exists between language construction and the relation of a singularity to the common. The common is never a unity, unless this is understood in terms of global meaning. Conversely, singularities are never primary elements except as expressions. And only the entire process, that is, the structure of relations, really constitutes the common.

Consequently, this conception of the production of subjectivity impels us *to revise our concept of constituent power*. In this perspective, constituent power is not simply linked to constitution (the temporality of the event and the form of insurrection); it is also linked to *the continuous and determined ontological construction of the common*. Through this ontological construction, we believe it is possible to use the entirety of Foucault's teachings and give them political weight—a weight that Foucault strongly emphasized in his last years, in particular when he considered the possibility of a biopolitical transformation of bodies at the intersection of passions and language.

We are thus in a condition we might perfectly define as an *Aufklärung* of bodies, in which political subjectivity is constituted by the doubling of subjectivity into a singular body and a common project.

Through our analysis, we have been able to locate a progressive (and discontinuous) action of political subjectivity tending, in all cases, towards the common. The movement of singularities and that of being coincide in this tendency, since the common is not an organic reality but an intermixing of singularities, an expression of freedom. Of course, we find ourselves before a paradox that is somehow implied by the idea of becoming-multitude (*faire*-multitude): discontinuities and doublings, jumps and continuity, power (*puissance*) and tendency are forms under which the political—as ontological ground and voluntary decision—nevertheless succeeds in reaching its own end, one that is not, however, a *telos*. The very matter of this strong yet haphazard development, ateleological and yet absolutely signifying, is the construction of the common. Thus, constituent power and the production of common freedom become terms, even if they are not univocally interchangeable, that tend towards it.

The long development that corresponds to the *political construction of subjectivity* (or, more precisely, to the *production of political subjectivity*, that is, to *becoming-multitude*) stems, in reality, from the great paradox we call "poverty." By poverty, we do not mean simple physical and material destitution, that is, a simple condition of deprivation, but the need to develop relations and cooperation in order to supplement a state of lack and deprivation. We are not affirming that all states of absolute destitution succeed in producing the common, but that the natural, historical, and social constraints weighing on singularities can give rise to infinite possibilities of action that the necessity, or better yet, the will to escape this infinite need allow.

In reality, it seems that the production of a common subjectivity is permitted when *two fundamental forces* come into contact. We have just spoken of the first one: we might call it, using a classical metaphor, the "force of poverty." This force is established based on an ontological discontinuity that emerges at a given moment: a moment of nonbeing tending towards the absolute, a need that opens up to power (*puissance*), a desire that can no longer be repressed. The strength of poverty is the strength to jump above the categories to which the human condition is initially predisposed. Sometimes, it is a jump into emptiness, and over emptiness. It implies taking a risk, but always carries with it the totality of imaginable life choices and/or choices of liberation. This is why we can call this force a "*potentia*" in the Spinozan sense of the word.

There must consequently exist a diachronic and temporal path that leads from poverty to the ontological construction of the common. Spinoza described this when he showed the continuity of *cupiditas* (as love, that is, as the *desire to develop potentia* that the subject, if poor, carries within) in relation to *conatus* (as poverty, as the original attempt to conserve one's own life). *We can see how it is possible to go from the first force—poverty—to the second—love.* As is the case with poverty, the term "love" must be understood both at a repetition of the classical (Platonic) metaphor of love, and its reversal. If need and love were organically linked for Plato, on the contrary, we must here understand the productive continuity—

and, paradoxically, the ontological jump—that permits the passage from one to the other.

We thus arrive at an absolutely positive turning point, since poverty means the tension, *the opening towards a possible increase of being.* Clearly, the simple allusion to the discontinuity of the processes of bodies and/or of the common was not enough to give us a genuine perspective of openness, all it did was accentuate our malaise. On the contrary, the rediscovery of poverty and love as forces, that is, as powers (*puissances*), gives us a glimpse of an affirmative line of flight based on passions, a passage through being itself, showing us the materialization of the *telos* that the becoming-multitude constructs. This is precisely what must help us ascribe continuity to becoming-multitude (a theoretical continuity for philosophy, an intellectual and militant one for movements). For the common must now appear as the product of a dynamics taking shape from the "inside," one that cannot be reduced to a dialectical schema, and affirms itself as an instance of recomposition. In reality, it is the mobile figure of *the action of love through poverty.*

Whenever we speak of love, we must absolutely exclude its romantic and theological definitions. These are responsible for a violent castration of the ontological dimension of love. By excluding them, we shall also avoid irony and gross misunderstandings.

On the one hand, we refuse all references to romantic inter-pretations and to the isolation that the word love had to accept. From this point of view, pornography—we are thinking of Georges Bataille's extraordinary thought—might be a perfect epitaph, and erotic individualism might represent its genuine substance! This is not at all what we understand by love.

On the other hand, we must also refuse all theological definitions of love. Here as well, genuine love is concealed and destroyed within a mystical, finalist, and neutralizing dimension that no longer recognizes any possibility of creation and ends up eliminating love itself. From Walter Benjamin to Jean-Luc Nancy, we can thus recognize in contemporary thought a mystic vein searching for a community foundation so as to guarantee its own analysis of politics. This is incorrect, and is unfortunately beyond correcting as well.

The concept of poverty needs to be demystified in the same way. There again, we are faced with two fundamental, and misleading interpretations.

The first interprets poverty as an irreducible and nonmodifiable object at the heart of a process that is in reality the religious affirmation of divine power. Poverty gives rise to pity. It is the sign of our impossibility to restore the absolute plenitude of Being. It is the indelible mark of original sin, a projection in the history of man of the sin that soils him.

The second interpretation we must fight against can be qualified as economist and socialist. In this case, the poor are unproductive and do not participate in the power (*puissance*) of the common (defined, as the case may be, as the common of the class, of the nation, etc.).

How can we attribute any truth-value to these two conceptions—one religious, the other socialist—at a time when the transformations of labor show us the way in which a "poor naturality" is now the essential form of production, cooperation and communication? How does the gift relation (as Mauss spoke of it) present itself today as a "productive gift"—an essential place of innovation in cognitive, social, relational, and linguistic work?

The content of the production of political and democratic subjectivity is thus starting to take on a radically new form. The question is not to find a common foundation, preestablished, objective, that would always have existed in the materiality of social relations. On the contrary, and mostly, we are looking to construct a dynamics of association of singularities in the common. We are speaking of a development from the "bottom up," going from absolute need (poverty) to the absolute gift (love) through pathways that are always ontological and material. What we are doing here is simply rendering *diachronically, in postmodernity,* what Spinoza had described *synchronically, in modernity*: the movement that leads from the individual need to democratic society.

We have thus arrived at the necessary apology of work and power as complementary figures of *dynamis*: not from an abstract point of view but in the intimate interlacing of networks of social production. As we have seen, in the current situation, the concept of power itself—administration, jurisdiction, etc.— is diluted within the different articulations of discontinuity and doubling. On the level of this line of resistance, it seems difficult to think of the exercise of power under the classic form attributed to it and under which it is generally described. If we consider the new conditions of becoming-multitude or becoming-political (*faire-politique*) that we have described, we can deduce that such management of power must be measured antagonistically against a new perspective: *the exercise of the common*. Where new subjectivities appear, a new exercise of power must necessarily be analyzed.

Perhaps we can now conduct *a radical revision of the concept of power*. It is considered not as a monolithic reality but as a partial and biased force that is just as incapable of realizing itself through all of its own tensions as it is paralyzed by the nostalgia of the monarchic character of *archè* that has always marked its expression. The concept of power presents itself according to an ideological dimension and to a historical continuity that have become completely obsolete. Just as Bodin could say that any form of government was monarchical (inasmuch as the One always characterized sovereignty in the modern period), we can today affirm that *the form of government and the substance of power are reducible to Two*, that is, to a coupling of forces and a confrontation of different *potentias. It is the exercise of the common against the exercise of power.* When we must define sovereignty, this is the transcendental conflict that we find everywhere in the passage from the modern to the postmodern.

Hic Rhodus, his salta. We believe we have accepted the fight.

Conclusion

This series of conferences took the form of an open research project. These workshops were meant to provide instruments, pose problems, formulate hypotheses, and open new fields of enquiry in order to elaborate a new postmodern political lexicon. We started by emphasizing the caesura between modernity and postmodernity, and went on to examine the genesis of biopolitics, this new framework that all politicophilosophical themes must henceforth confront.

We then inquired into the double crisis of the modern state that globalization has provoked: on the one hand, the emancipation of the colonies (and the consequent reformulation of notions of mobility and borders), on the other, the confrontation of modern sovereignty with new forms of sovereignty that the globalization of administration and imperial domination demand.

Finally, we then analyzed a number of postmodern political philosophies, trying to concentrate on the sometimes absolutely acritical and unproductive elements they presented. On this question, we are convinced that these postmodern theories, even if they sometimes clearly identified the caesura separating them from modernity, could never go beyond a kind of marginality. And inversely, we believe their ontology is unable to position its own source of resistance and transformation at the heart of the mutation that demands our attention.

Our own position developed from the critique of these positions. We suggested that the emergence of a right to resistance, a constituent power, and a new subjective right that has become multitudinous *potentia* must be detected neither on the margins nor *outside* the actual configuration of systems of power, but instead at their heart, internally, on the *inside*. We had to justify this position by negative argumentation, that is, by analyzing a number of concepts such as government, governance, Empire, and sovereignty in a critical manner, pinpointing the new aporias appearing in the postmodern and globalized context. We then tried to recompose, in a positive, propositive, and affirmative manner, the horizon of this social transformation so intimately linked today to the ontological specificities of the production of subjectivity.

We therefore had to stop at a second series of notions—but also practices, experiences, projects—that corresponded to the theme of "decision," "organization," and "communism." In reality, it was within an entirely redefined temporality that we had to ascertain the novel relation between resistance and the construction of a new world, between the exercise of counter-power and the exercise of the common.

If we speak of temporality today, we invoke two different meanings, both completely new in relation to the ontological determinations of modernity. The first dimension of temporality is that of history: time is present there as an internal, centripetal rupture, or as a transition, a sort of democratic "Old Regime." But time is also a tension towards this absolute democracy that must be constructed in life, in the biopolitical experience of our present existence.

This transition is quite dramatic in many regards, as it opposes the rigidity of certain modern concepts with the living *potentias* of the postmodern. In this case, we cannot bet on an ethics of responsibility, on the respect of the values of a community whose preestablished existence we are supposing. In the transition towards the postmodern, responsibility (and the ethical behavior that follows suit) must confront crisis and innovation with the understanding that both are necessary. There is no other way.

However, along with a clear perception of the crisis underlying the transition comes a second perception of time, one that no longer plays on history but on ontology. Faced with the uncertainty and the difficulty of overcoming this obstacle, this conception shows the punctual dimension of the decision at hand: if the consciousness of the transition forced us to look backwards, the *kairos* of decision necessitates a forward gaze.

Undoubtedly, idealists might find this tension intolerable: only by delving into real temporality can we get to the bottom of the problem and loosen the knot that is paralyzing our thinking. It will then be possible to make *virtus* and *fortuna* coincide—according to the *kairos*, this represents perhaps the possibility of reaching truth. Heidegger was probably right in telling us that we had to immerse ourselves wholeheartedly in the ontological materiality of temporality in order to overcome the crisis befalling—and embodying—the transition. Yet he was wrong to consider this delving to be fated, without issue, and to make Being a weight on our shoulders (or a rock to hang from our necks, so as to better sink into the sea of Being). He was also wrong when he considered our despair faced with the passage of time that opens onto nothingness, faced with this nothingness crisscrossing our existence at every moment, faced, finally, with the poverty racking the human condition. He was wrong because this ontological delving into temporality, into despair and poverty, is immediately transfigured by love understood as an ontological power (*puissance*): it becomes fundamental for the production of a political subjectivity as well as for the production of riches. It is along this extreme limit running between poverty and love that we claim for humanity the Spinozan capacity of constructing a new democracy. *To become the multitude is to become democracy.*

SEMIOTEXT(E) Post-Political Politics

AUTONOMIA
Post-Political Politics
Edited by Sylvère Lotringer and Christian Marazzi

Semiotext(e) is reissuing, in book form, its legendary magazine issue *Autonomia: Post-Political Politics*, originally published in New York in 1980. Edited by Sylvère Lotringer and Christian Marazzi with the direct participation of the main leaders and theorists of the Autonomist movement (including Antonio Negri, Mario Tronti, Franco Piperno, Oreste Scalzone, Paolo Virno, Sergio Bologna, and Franco Berardi), this volume is the only first-hand document and contemporaneous analysis that exists of the most innovative post-'68 radical movement in the West.

7 x 10 • 340 pages • ISBN: 978-1-58435-053-8 • $24.95

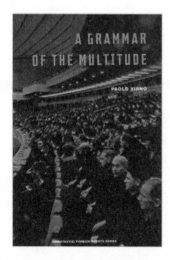

A GRAMMAR OF THE MULTITUDE
Paolo Virno, Translated by Isabella Bertoletti, James Cascaito and Andrea Casson

Globalization is forcing us to rethink some of the categories—such as "the people"—that traditionally have been associated with the now eroding state. Italian political thinker Paolo Virno argues that the category of "multitude," elaborated by Spinoza and for the most part left fallow since the seventeenth century, is a far better tool to analyze contemporary issues than the Hobbesian concept of "people," favored by classical political philosophy.

Drawing from philosophy of language, political economics, and ethics, Virno shows that being foreign, "not-feeling-at-home-anywhere," is a condition that forces the multitude to place its trust in the intellect. In conclusion, Virno suggests that the metamorphosis of the social systems in the West during the last twenty years is leading to a paradoxical "Communism of the Capital."

6 x 9 • 120 pages • ISBN: 978-1-58435-021-7 • $14.95

Paolo Virno

MULTITUDE

BETWEEN INNOVATION
AND NEGATION

<e>

MULTITUDE BETWEEN INNOVATION AND NEGATION

Paolo Virno, Translated by Isabella Bertoletti, James Cascaito and Andrea Casson

Multitude between Innovation and Negativity offers three essays that take the reader on a journey through the political philosophy of language.

"Wit and Innovative Action" explores the ambivalence inevitably arising when the semiotic and the semantic, grammar and experience, rule and regularity, and right and fact intersect. "Mirror Neurons, Linguistic Negation, and Mutual Recognition" examines the relationship of language and intersubjective empathy: without language, would human beings be able to recognize other members of their species? And finally, in "Multitude and Evil," Virno challenges the distinction between the state of nature and civil society and argues for a political institution that resembles language in its ability to be at once nature and history.

6 x 9 • 200 pages • ISBN: 978-1-58435-050-7 • $14.95

Christian Marazzi

CAPITAL
AND LANGUAGE

FROM THE NEW ECONOMY TO THE WAR ECONOMY

<e>

CAPITAL AND LANGUAGE
From the New Economy to the War Economy
Christian Marazzi, Translated by Gregory Conti
Introduction by Michael Hardt

Capital and Language focuses on the causes behind the international economic and financial depression of 2001, and on the primary instrument that the U.S. government has since been using to face them: war. Marazzi points to capitalism's fourth stage (after mercantilism, industrialism, and the post-Fordist culmination of the New Economy): the "War Economy" that is already upon us.

Marazzi offers a radical new understanding of the current international economic stage and crucial post-Marxist guidance for confronting capitalism in its newest form.

6 x 9 • 180 pages • ISBN: 978-1-58435-067-5 • $14.95